Second Marriage in the Catholic Church

Second Marriage in the Catholic Church

'Annulment' and other Solutions

Paul Robbins

Copyright © 2019 Paul Robbins
All rights reserved
ISBN 9781791753153

Dedication

Dedicated to all who have shared their marital histories in pursuit of a declaration of nullity. Your stories have assisted in the writing of this book.

Table of Contents

Preface ix

SECTION I 1
Chapter 1   The Church's Approach to Marriage Breakdown . 2
Chapter 2   The Nature of Marriage 7
Chapter 3   Marriage and Vocation 12
Chapter 4   Marriage and the Law of the Church 18
Chapter 5   What is a Declaration of Nullity? 22
Chapter 6   Lawful Manifestation 29
Chapter 7   Legal Capability 34
Chapter 8   Consent 40
Chapter 9   Grave Lack of Discretionary Judgement 45
Chapter 10 Inability 62
Chapter 11 Error and Fraud 72
Chapter 12 Defects of Intention 76
Chapter 13 Other Defects of Consent 83

SECTION II 87
Chapter 14 The Tribunal System 88
Chapter 15 The Petitioner 93
Chapter 16 The Respondent 101
Chapter 17 Providing Proof of Nullity 108
Chapter 18 Concluding the Process 114
Chapter 19 Judgement and Appeal 118
Chapter 20 The Briefer Process 123
Chapter 21 Other Matters Pertinent to the Nullity Process .. 127

SECTION III 133
Chapter 22 Marriage Dissolution in the Church 134
Chapter 23 The Internal Forum Solution 137
Glossary of Terms 152

Preface

Despite its firm teaching about the permanence of marriage, many people whose marriages have ended prematurely are able to remarry in the Catholic Church.

In the recent past, society's understanding of marriage has undergone a significant change. Many countries have changed their laws to allow for the possibility that two people of the same gender can form a marriage. The history of the human race before that time, however, was that marriage was possible only between a man and a woman.

The history of marriage in Biblical teachings suggests that God created marriage at the same time as he created man and woman. These teachings substantially determined the nature of marriage over thousands of years. Such teachings were seen as coming from God and so incapable of change, until recently. The Christian Churches, however, continue to teach that marriage is possible only between one man and one woman because that is the teaching found in the Bible. That doesn't mean that other relationships do not have value.

It is this traditional model of marriage that is the subject of this book. Specifically, the book concerns itself only with marriage as understood by the Roman Catholic Church. It examines the remedies available to those whose marriages did not last until the death of one of the spouses.

'Annulment' is the common but inappropriate word often used of one solution to a desire to remarry. The Catholic Church does not annul marriages. To do that would imply there had been a true marriage and the Church was denying or changing that truth. The Church has no authority to change God's truth. What the Church does is declare some marriages to have been null, which means they are and always were null; in other words, a true marriage was not formed on the wedding day.

Many commonly-held beliefs concerning Catholic Church 'annulments' are wrong. These include: that they are available only to the rich or famous; that they make children of the marriage illegitimate; that any marriage celebrated in a register office can be annulled; and, that they are only possible when a marriage is not consummated. The reality is that many marriages that have ended prematurely are capable of being declared null. Successfully applying for a declaration of nullity of a marriage in Church law can assist a person to live in peace with God in a second marriage, knowing with confidence that something essential to true marriage was missing from the first.

The possibility of having a marriage declared null has been part of the practice of the Church for many centuries. One of the factors that sparked the Reformation movement in England in the 16th century was the refusal of the Vatican to grant King Henry VIII a declaration of nullity of his marriage to his first wife, Catherine of Aragon.

In 2015, Pope Francis amended the provisions of Church

law that deal specifically with the marriage nullity process. He introduced a shorter process for those few marriages that appear obviously null. He also made other changes that should reduce the time it takes to process many cases. He wanted to ensure that, if a marriage is invalid, it can be declared as such quickly.

There is nothing contained in this book that contradicts the teachings and discipline of the Catholic Church. Indeed, the practices outlined here lend support to the Church's teaching that marriage is a permanent partnership of conjugal life and love that has as its ends the well-being of the couple and the procreation and upbringing of children (cf. Vatican II, *Gaudium et Spes*, n.48). It is certain that many marriages fall far short of this and Church teaching can lack conviction if it does not reflect reality. Hence, that the Church has the facility to declare null and void a marriage that never succeeded in being a 'partnership of conjugal life and love' lends credibility to its teaching and its desire to portray what is inherently known to many; that marriage is a good and desirable institution.

This book starts from some basic premises, briefly examining the Church's approach to marriage breakdown and its teaching concerning marriage, before introducing the concept of marriage nullity and the reasons a marriage might be declared null. It then explains the processes used by the Church before, finally, examining what might happen when a formal solution is not available.

SECTION I

Chapter 1

The Church's Approach to Marriage Breakdown

For those who believe that marriage is for life, and this is particularly true for those who align themselves with a Church that continually affirms the permanent nature of marriage, the breakdown of their own marriage can feel like alienation from God. Sometimes such people choose simply to remain separated from their spouses rather than seek divorce. Some do this because of their belief in the biblical teaching from Jesus that divorce is not acceptable.

Others, however, find that legal separation is not enough. For those who see divorce as contrary to the teachings of Jesus, it is worthwhile reflecting on His teaching in its context. Jesus stated that nobody can divide what God has united. He went on to state that any man who divorces his wife and marries another is guilty of adultery, as is any woman who divorces her husband and marries another (cf. Mark 10:1-12).

Jesus speaks of divorce as the division of something that God has united. When remarriage follows the division of this God-made union, then the guilt of adultery occurs.

Thus, it is in the context of remarriage that Jesus focuses on divorce. It is in this context that He refers to divorce as sin. He does not say that divorce is a sin when remarriage does not occur after divorce.

However, what is of great significance is that Jesus refers to the spiritual dimension of marriage; something God has made. He sees it as a part of God's plan. It follows from this that the bond is permanent. God has created that bond and so no one can divide it. The question arises: for any particular marriage, how can we know if God has or has not united these two people in marriage; after all, people have free will?

The Catholic Church's discipline as regards the permanence of marriage focuses on this teaching of Jesus and so presumes that, when two people take part in a wedding ceremony, God unites them in marriage. Hence, the Church's position with respect to all marriages is that they are to be considered as true marriages, unless it might be shown otherwise.

The Catholic Church presumes that God unites all who exchange consent in a wedding ceremony and therefore it is not possible for anyone to remarry while his or her spouse is still alive. Yet, who can know the mind of God? As will be shown, it can be said with certainty that not everyone who exchanges consent to marriage actually succeeds in becoming married. To put it another way, not every wedding produces a marriage. If a marriage does not result from a particular wedding ceremony and the man and woman later separate or divorce, how can it be said that they are dividing that which God has united?

Divorce is often the only realistic option after spouses have separated permanently and Jesus does not appear to condemn divorce simply because a marital relationship became unsustainable.

Divorce is not recognised in Catholic Church law, known as canon law. This law is written in separate statements known as canons. The Code of canon law is the collection of canons.

Law has played a part in the relationship between God and people since time immemorial. Examples of early law can be seen in the command of God to Adam not to eat from the tree of the knowledge of good and evil (Genesis 2:17) and God gave to Moses the ten commandments (cf. Exodus, ch. 20). Since its institution by Christ, the Church has issued laws but it was not until 1917 that the Catholic Church gathered these various laws together into the first Code of canon law. Following the Second Vatican Council, canon law was substantially revised and the principal body of law now governing the Roman Catholic Church is the 1983 Code of canon law, with its subsequent amendments.

The Code of canon law does not mention divorce. Divorce is a matter of civil or secular law and so Catholics who are divorced are recognised as free to remarry in secular law but, since Catholics are also bound to observe canon law, they are still considered bound by the promises they made before God and the Church.

So, what is the Church's position on the subjects of marital separation and divorce? On the subject of marriage separation, canon law recognises certain situations in which one spouse can lawfully leave the other. Adultery is specifically mentioned in the Code as a justifiable reason for separation, as is any situation when staying together might result in grave danger to the soul or body of a spouse or one of the children. However, the Code goes further and embraces every possible and reasonable circumstance in which separation might occur because it states that separation is possible when simply living together becomes too difficult. Thus, although the Church has taken a firm stance on the permanence of marriage, the law of the Church recognises that situations arise in which separation of those who are married is justified. Nevertheless, even when separation occurs, the Church continues to recognise the spouses as bound to one another by the promises they made on the wedding day. The bond of their marriage remains and they are not considered free to attempt another marriage.

Divorce is the dissolution of a marriage bond; it brings a marriage to an end. Thus, a marriage existed but ceases to exist in secular law when the legal document that is a divorce decree is issued. Since the Church does not accept that divorce is possible, canon law has nothing to say about it because dissolution of a marriage bond, whilst recognised by the law as possible in some limited circumstances (see Chapter 22), does not otherwise occur in the Catholic Church.

Since canon law and civil or secular law are distinct and separate, a Catholic who refers to himself or herself as divorced is always speaking of a divorce granted only in secular law. A secular law divorce can have only secular law effects, and it is for those secular law effects, such as distribution of assets and custody of children, that many seek divorce. This breaking of the secular law bond of marriage has no effect on the canonical bond, which continues in existence. Whether or not the canonical bond accords with reality is examined more fully in Chapter 4.

Secular divorce carries with it an implied inherent right to remarriage and it is primarily this that the Church does not accept because it is contrary to the teaching given to us by Jesus. The Church, by including provisions in canon law whereby married couples can separate, simply recognises the reality that some married couples find greater peace by living apart than by being together.

As with many tragedies in life, it is difficult to appreciate the traumatic effects of marriage breakdown without actually suffering them. Some compare marital breakdown to bereavement in that, when the marriage fails, a part of the self also dies. Whatever was the state of the relationship, the breakdown is still the final shattering of hopes and dreams and perhaps an admission of failure, possibly even when there is no fault. It represents the transition from one way of life to another that is completely different. It is important to realise that marriage breakdown for a believer is unlikely to have occurred without considerable soul-searching and divorce will have been a last resort. For a believer, such decisions are not made without prayer, thought and openness to God through conscience.

The remaining chapters in this first section will explain how a second marriage can be possible for some by obtaining a declaration that the first union was not a valid marriage. This cannot realistically be understood without an understanding of marriage. A brief summary of the Church's teaching on the nature of marriage is the subject matter of the next chapter.

Chapter 2

The Nature of Marriage

The Church teaches the important role that marriage plays in family life and society in general. In the face of so many marriages breaking down, Church teaching also emphasises the permanent nature of marriage. After all, if a marriage is God-made, the couple are walking their path to salvation and the Church is doing nothing more than urging the couple to be faithful to God's call to them. That is the mission of the Church.

The Church's teaching about marriage has shifted in emphasis in the last hundred years. The Church used to teach that the primary purpose of marriage was the continuance of the human race; that is, it created a stable environment into which children could be born and raised. Its primary purpose was, therefore, viewed as procreative. If the marital relationship proved to be also good for the spouses, this was secondary. Now, however, the Catholic Church teaches that marriage has two objects, neither of which is primary: the marital partnership is both for the good of the spouses and for the procreation and education of children. Out of these teachings flows the possibilities for declaring a marriage to have been invalid or not a true marriage.

In the documents of the Second Vatican Council, marriage is described as a covenant. The word 'covenant' was used in the Old Testament to describe the relationship between God and His chosen people. It was founded in the phrase "You will be my people and I will be your God" (Jeremiah 7:23). There was an understanding between God and His people that He would watch over them provided they kept His laws. With the coming of Jesus, a new covenant is formed that is linked to the old. Jesus, by His death on the cross, becomes the mediator between God and His people. Now, in the new covenant, believers are asked by God to "love one another as I have loved you" (John 13:34).

Saint Paul tells us that this new covenant is the example of love to be copied by married couples. In the letter to the Ephesians, he presents God's message according to the customs of the time. He tells husbands to love their wives "just as Christ loved the Church and sacrificed himself for her"; in other words, to make a gift of their whole selves. He also tells wives to submit to their husbands, which again is an expression of total self-gift (cf. Ephesians 5:15-20). Jesus gave his life for the Church. It was a total gift and is the supreme example of the way Christians should approach marriage: the giving of one's life to another person for his or her good. True marriage is the mutual self-gift of two persons and, of course, the acceptance of that gift of each by the other. It is, in a very real and full sense, two becoming one.

This teaching of the Church about marriage is also expressed in Pope Paul VI's encyclical, *Humanae Vitae*. He sets the marital union in the context of God's plan for mankind. It is, he says, the realisation of 'His design of love' (cf. *Humanae Vitae*, n.8).

Pope Paul VI describes the gift of husband and wife to one another as 'the reciprocal personal gift of self'. This is the essence of the marital relationship and that which distinguishes it from other relationships. In *Familiaris Consortio* (n. 11), Pope John Paul II referred to the total physical self-gift of the sexual act as a lie unless it was an expression of the total personal self-gift which is marriage. In *Amoris Laetitia*, Pope Francis reflects on the Hebrew word used in the bible for the joining together of a man and woman in marriage, saying it speaks of a profound harmony, both physical and interior, and he says the same word is used to describe our union with God (cf. n. 13).

This total and unreserved self-gift of the whole person to the spouse forms the essence of a true marriage and enables that partnership of the whole of life to be formed. Yet, in reality, a marriage is formed by two people who bring into that union their individual faults, failings and imperfections. In order to form a true marriage, the partners are called to orientate their lives towards that mutual donation and acceptance.

This gift of one spouse to the other does not mean that husband and wife must deny their individuality. People cannot change their personalities to accommodate marriage and any attempt at such is likely to lead to eventual unhappiness. Anyone entering marriage has to accept the other as he or she is, 'warts and all'. There are some who attempt marriage expecting to change the other. That is a mistake. It won't happen. Spouses will naturally express their individuality within the context of the relationship. The commitment of the whole of life to another person can only succeed in being a true marriage if each adopts that disposition that puts the well-being of both at the centre of their lives. In the interpersonal relationship that forms the basis of true marriage, the unconditional love of each for the other will not stifle the individuality of the other but allow him or her to grow in an atmosphere of love, acceptance and care that fosters a willingness to reciprocate that self-gift.

It is to be hoped that the courtship period will be a time during which a couple can learn to appreciate the effect individual interests, such as the sport or hobbies to which one of them is particularly attached, may have on any future they wish to make together. There will also, of necessity, be some individual pursuits that enhance the marriage; the daily work of one or both is an obvious example. It can also happen that the couple will find that some leisure time spent apart enhances their marriage. The gift of the whole of life to the other in marriage simply means that the spouses should give a higher priority to their relationship than to their individual wishes.

Hence, the nature of this relationship sets marriage apart from two people who are simply cohabiting; people who decide to live together, rather than making a commitment such as marriage. They may share the same roof over their heads, a car, a bed, meals and even much of their leisure time. They may share some finances and even be parents of the same child(ren). Yet, unless they have made that unreserved gift of self to the other, and have expressed that in the giving of consent, they have not entered the state of matrimony.

The gift of self in marriage is a gift without reservation

and it can only be such a gift if it lasts until the death of one of the parties. In other words, the permanence of marriage flows naturally from its essence as an unreserved self-gift.

This permanent aspect of marriage is both awesome and wonderful. It is awesome in its implications of exclusivity, forsaking all others and yet wonderful in the elements of trust, friendship and respect that can develop. If marriage is seen as temporary, the partners are likely to withhold some element of themselves from the partnership, if for no other reason than a fear of being hurt should the other decide to leave. It seems that some people today are marrying with no sense of commitment to the other person or with no expectation that they will still be together in a few years. Such an approach is far removed from the nature of true marriage as forming a partnership based on total self-gift.

The process of two becoming one is the on-going task of marriage. Those who fail to realise that – they perhaps give up trying after the wedding day – have failed to understand the nature of marriage as a gift of self. The taking of the other expressed on the wedding day is possible only if the other makes that gift of self; and the essence of marriage is the day-to-day give and take – the "reciprocal personal gift of self", as Pope Paul VI called it. The essence of marriage is found in the daily manifestation of selfless giving to the other. That is the covenant: the ceaseless attempting to enhance the good of the other, whilst also receiving that gift from the other. Unless that desire to make a gift of self to the other underlies the decision to marry, the potential for marital failure must be present.

Chapter 3

Marriage and Vocation

If, as people of faith, we accept God's uniting work in marriage, it has to be right for couples who plan to marry to discern if their decision accords with the will of God. This is true both for their happiness in this life and for their ultimate salvation.

How can a couple be sure that what they are doing is God's will; in other words, that they are entering a God-made union? In truth, we can rarely be certain that any action corresponds with the will of God. We can only attempt to evaluate the proposed course of action over a period of time and then, if things appear right, take a leap of faith. There are certain guidelines that can help in that discernment, but they can never prevent mistakes being made.

Jesus tells us that God knows each one of us intimately. In

the gospel of St. Matthew (6:6), Jesus says that God sees all that is done in secret. In the gospel of St. Luke (12:7), He makes the statement that every hair on our heads is known to God. In the gospel of St. John (1:45,47-49) is found the story of Nathanael meeting Jesus for the first time. Jesus refers to him as an Israelite who is incapable of deceit, thus indicating that Jesus already knows Nathanael intimately.

If we can accept that God knows each one of us in this way, we can begin to realise that each of us is unique in His eyes and that each has a part to play in His plan. We may try to discover what that part is, but it may be a life-long search that can produce unexpected results. In marriage, for example, the actual coming together in a wedding ceremony is just one step on a journey; a journey that requires a continuous and life-long seeking by one spouse to work with the other to enhance the well-being of both. Together they can discover if they are called to be parents, of one or perhaps more children with varying abilities and perhaps disabilities, the values, care and general education they will give those children and in what way their marriage can bring benefit to their families and the wider community outside the immediate family. It can happen that one of the spouses will die before old age and the other might be called to remarry or to give himself or herself in service of others in a way that may not have been possible if the marriage had continued.

How can a couple know if God is calling them to form a marriage together? Usually, the most appropriate guide to discovering God's calling to us is in understanding ourselves and the deepest desires within us. God's call for each of us is a fundamental part of who we are. His calling to each of us is found within the unique person – me – He created. As we grow in knowledge of ourselves, as we learn about our strengths and weaknesses, each of us gradually comes to some awareness of what it is and what it is not possible for us to do with our lives and, particularly, what we want to do with our lives; what it is that will give us a deep sense of fulfilment.

It is these particular desires, the deepest desires of my being, that are the best guide to God's call for me. The idea that God, who is love, would call any of us to a life of unhappiness is unthinkable. His call to each person is that way of life that is most compatible with that person's being. Such a way of life will lead to an interior contentment and a sense of a life well-lived. This is most often found in the service of others, perhaps in the role of spouse, parent, carer or in some other way, such as providing for the needs of others through one's paid work, that contributes to the good of one or more others.

In determining God's calling for me, feelings are very important. There is a danger of over-simplifying a complex topic and only some basic principles can be mentioned here. Generally speaking, an action that is compatible with the essence of my being will lead to a feeling of contentment, a deep-felt awareness that the action is right and an inner peace. Likewise, an action that is incompatible with my being will leave an uncomfortable feeling; perhaps a pang of conscience; a feeling of 'this is not me'; an awareness that something is wrong; general anxiety. These are not the momentary feelings of happiness, sadness, joy, pain, frustration or any of the thousand different feelings we experience naturally every day. It might be exciting to steal a bar of chocolate and a delight to consume it, but my deeper awareness is that the act of theft was wrong (cf. Proverbs 20:17). Connecting with these deeper feelings and desires is not always easy.

The person who lives a life in accordance with God's will – that is according to his or her vocation – will experience over time an air of peace and contentment from within, no matter what trials and tribulations might come in everyday life (cf. the warning contained in the reward for those who follow Jesus: Mark 10:28-31). Likewise, the person who is trying to live a life that is not in accordance with the will of God will experience over time deep-seated anxiety or disturbance. It is often said of those who are wicked: I don't know how they live with themselves. This is precisely the point being made.

These aids to finding God's will are as appropriate to marriage as to any other vocation. When Jesus referred to that which God has united, he implied that the woman and man are responding to God's call. In an ideal world, this would be true of all marriages. In reality, however, people marry for many reasons, not all of which might be interpreted as a response to God's call to form a marriage as understood by the Church.

Those who speak of their decision to marry as 'it felt right', or 'we loved one another in a way that we had never experienced before', or 'we couldn't imagine living the rest of our lives without one another', or 'we just knew we were good for one another' might be said to have been responding to a call from God. Those who appeared to marry only because she was pregnant by him, because he liked that she earned a lot of money, because they enjoyed a good sexual relationship or because it gave each the opportunity to get away from home, might still have responded to God's call – His ways must never be underestimated – but might also be entering a union that was never any part of God's plan. Such motives can have implications for grounds for nullity, as will be explained later.

It is important that inappropriate conclusions are not drawn from this. It might give an impression that those in happy marriages have been united by God and those in unhappy marriages have not. Individual free will and the possibility of sin can render a true marriage unhappy. Also, a man and a woman, after their wedding, might happily live separate lives without ever making that gift of self that would render their union a marriage in the true sense of the word. As they are individually happy in their situation, their so-called marriage can survive.

Permanence is part of the very nature of marriage; that is, it flows from the very nature of the totality of the gift of self that the marriage covenant demands. Hence, it would be a most serious matter for a true marriage to break down. For what has happened in marriage breakdown – and this is referring only to true marriages, by which is meant marriages in which that unreserved gift has been made by both partners such that they have established an appropriate partnership of life – is that the marriage has taken a course that is contrary to its own nature. It might be said that, if something is truly united by God, He is likely to have used a kind of spiritual super-glue to hold it together. Hence, for a true marriage to break down, it must have happened that one or both of the parties took some action, perhaps unwittingly, that amounted to a withdrawal of the gift of self made on the wedding day. If that has not happened and the marriage has broken down, it must be possible that there never was a true marriage.

Many communities in the world, for different reasons, consider it important to attach some rules and regulations to the marital state. In many countries, for example, formal registration of a marriage is required in order for it to be recognised. In that respect, the Church is no different. A study of the Church's approach to the law that governs marriage in the Church is helpful to an understanding of declarations of nullity of marriage and is the subject of the next chapter.

Chapter 4

Marriage and the Law of the Church

Marriage is first of all a natural institution and so those elements of it that might be described as of natural law, that which flows from the nature of things, apply to everyone whatever might be their faith. Within the Catholic Church, marriage is also governed by canon law.

As with any society or organisation, the Church has a need to establish structures and create order for its effective working. Without this order, how would we know who was free to marry and who was not? How would we know what constituted a wedding ceremony such that a marriage was formed that the Church could recognise? How would we know if a child was old enough to enter marriage or a priest who has left the ministry was to be allowed to marry? How would we know if a woman or man whose marriage had ended in breakdown was to be allowed to try again?

The Church tries to ensure that there are adequate provisions and procedures in place to answer these questions. For example, it has already been noted that the Church, through canon law, presumes that all who exchange consent in a wedding ceremony have actually formed a marriage. Besides the need to protect the sanctity of marriage, this presumption seeks to prevent anyone from taking part in a wedding ceremony with one person and then trying to declare himself or herself unmarried or free to enter marriage with another person.

The Church has written many laws to safeguard marriage. Of the 1,752 canons of the 1983 Code of canon law, no less than 148 concern the subject of marriage. The principal areas covered by the canons are: the nature of marriage and the effects of marriage; those who can and cannot form a marriage; the procedures for forming a marriage and who may preside at a wedding ceremony; when and how the bond of marriage can be dissolved; and, separation of the spouses without dissolution of the bond of marriage. The Code also explains how marriages can be declared invalid and how invalid marriages can be convalidated; that is, be recognised as valid. Effectively then, the Church has taken a natural institution and tried to fit it within a legal structure. It is not a perfect fit.

When a couple take part in a wedding ceremony, either a marriage is formed or it is not. This truth is determined by the particular circumstances existing on the wedding day at the time of the exchange of consent. Whilst every reasonable step is taken to ensure that a marriage is formed, for example by trying to ensure that neither party is already bound in marriage to another, there is no guarantee that a marriage begins on the wedding day. The law, in its presumption that all marriages are valid, seeks both to assist the Church in its role of promoting Christ's teaching and to ensure order by presenting a uniform and stable legal base for marriage. Such order is required for the good of the whole community.

The preservation of order has wider implications that may not be recognised at first sight. A marriage is valid if all the essential legal conditions for its formation are fulfilled. If the marriage is valid, the man and woman become husband and wife. If an essential legal condition is not met, the marriage is invalid. That is a simple fact. The lack of fulfilment of that condition means a marriage was not formed, although canon law will presume that a marriage was formed. Hence, every wedding produces a legal marriage but it may or may not be a valid or true marriage.

It might not be known for several years, or indeed it may never be known, that an essential legal condition for the formation of a marriage was not met. Thus, the presumption that all marriages are valid assists in preventing any undue speculation, embarrassment or other unpleasantness that might otherwise have arisen from any doubt about the validity of a marriage. Even if it becomes certain that an essential condition was not met, the legal presumption of validity remains in place. This legal presumption only ceases if a declaration of marriage nullity is issued by Church authorities.

There is, then, an important distinction to be made between validity and legality. Validity is concerned with the essence of an action or state: does it exist; is it real? Legality is concerned only with the law's interpretation of the matter:

that is, does the law recognise it, irrespective of whether or not it actually exists? Thus, marriages are lawful if they are celebrated according to the requirements of the law. That is the only prerequisite for a lawful marriage. So, every public wedding is recognised as establishing a lawful marriage.

However, the validity of the marriage is only presumed. The presumption is that a true marriage was formed on the wedding day, whether or not a true marriage was actually formed. Whilst all possible steps are taken to try to ensure that a marriage is valid, that status is only ever presumed, since it is very difficult to know with any certainty if a valid marriage was actually formed.

The Church's laws regarding marriage are complex. Over the years, a framework of laws has been developed that tries to recognise both the sanctity of marriage and its form of a relationship of love between two people. The Church considers these laws to be of the utmost importance, affecting the very heart of marriage in such a way that, if certain laws are broken, the marriage simply does not come into existence. This is the starting point for an understanding of marriage nullity.

Chapter 5

What is a Declaration of Nullity?

A declaration of nullity is effectively a statement that something essential to the forming of a true marriage was missing on the wedding day. This usually occurs because one or both of the marriage partners did not, for one reason or another, make that necessary gift of self to the other. Hence, it is the approach of the spouses that is examined and grounds for nullity can be found in one or both spouses.

It is possible to recognise before the wedding that a proposed marriage has little chance of lasting, but it is often only after the parties have attempted to live as a married couple that the truth emerges. Consequently, it can happen that a marriage is declared invalid even when it appeared successful or has lasted for many years.

The concept of being able to remarry in the Church after having a marriage declared null can be difficult for some believers to accept. The first thing the Church teaches about marriage is that a bond is created that lasts until the death of one of the parties. However, there is nothing about nullity that contradicts this teaching. Nullity does not cancel or break that bond. Nullity declares that the marriage bond was never there; in other words, that a marriage never actually came into existence on the wedding day. A declaration of nullity is, if you like, a statement that the presumption that all marriages are valid does not hold true for the particular marriage that is declared null.

The Church permits the presumption of validity of marriage to be overturned by the production of proof that the marriage was not valid. If a marriage was not valid, then there was no marriage. The Church allows either spouse to challenge the presumption of validity of his/her marriage providing that the other spouse is still alive.

It does not matter if the spouse presenting the challenge to validity might have contributed to the breakdown of the marriage. In the event of the challenge to validity being upheld, a decree of nullity will be issued no matter which of the spouses presented the application.

It should be noted that it is not the pronouncement of invalidity by the Church that makes a marriage null but the circumstances that existed on the wedding day. The Church merely declares the marriage to have been invalid. Hence, the Church simply declares a historical fact; it cannot change that fact.

If this concept appears difficult, it might be useful to compare it with that of a man who enters a bank with a gun and steals a substantial sum of money. By the mere fact of that action, the man is a thief. Whether or not he is arrested, whether or not he is charged, whether or not he is convicted by a judge in court, he is in truth a thief. It is not the pronouncement of 'guilty' by a judge that makes him a thief, but the fact that he robbed the bank. It is the act of theft and not the court's pronouncement that determines the truth of whether or not he is a thief. The court's pronouncement of 'guilty' determines only his legal status and changes that status from 'presumed innocent' to 'guilty'. However, his innocence or guilt in truth is determined by the simple fact of whether or not he stole from the bank.

So it is with marriage nullity. It is the situation on the wedding day that determines the validity of the marriage. The truth of that situation cannot be changed by any pronouncement of the Church. Recognition of that truth and of the power of God to call people into marriage irrespective of the Church's determination of their canonical status means that nobody in the Church can rely on canonical status alone as a determination of truth. To preserve order for the good of the community, such status has to be respected but it should not be used as a basis for making moral judgements about people who are in new relationships after the failure of a previous marriage (for more on this, see Chapter 23).

A declaration of marriage nullity might be defined thus:

> A declaration of nullity is a declaration by competent authority that, at the time of the wedding, there was some (legal) defect that prevented the marriage coming into existence.

A marriage is the day-to-day fulfilment of the promises made on the wedding day. It is a living relationship of two people but it is not something easily identifiable as a marriage distinct from other relationships. To assist the public perception that a marriage has been created, its formation is manifested in a variety of ways, such as having a public ceremony, exchanging wedding rings, issuing a certificate and adopting the same last name. These signs help us to feel and believe that a marriage has begun, but they do not determine the existence of the marriage. On the wedding day, everyone behaves towards the couple and the couple relate to one another as though a marriage has been formed but nobody can prove that it has, because a marriage is not a tangible entity. The belief held by everybody on the wedding day and thereafter is false if the marriage is later declared invalid.

The written law plays a necessary role in these matters. When a wedding is celebrated, a marriage is recognised by the law whether or not a true marriage is formed. What constitutes a true marriage is what the law determines is required for the validity of that marriage. Hence, the law, in defining validity, also determines what might result in a marriage being declared invalid or null.

The nullity of the marriage can be declared only by competent authority. The law recognises as competent the diocesan bishop or the Holy Father or a person or body delegated with that authority, such as a diocesan judge. It is not possible for anyone else to declare the marriage to have been invalid. Again, those who are competent are defined by the law.

The declaration is given legal effect by means of a decree, which is a document signed by a competent person that has the effect of changing the legal status of the couple from married to unmarried, in the same way that a divorce decree does in secular law. As such, a decree of nullity is an important document and is usually retained by the diocese for safe-keeping. The fact of the declaration of nullity of the marriage will be communicated to the people who have charge of the registers of baptism or reception so that an entry can be made against the record of marriage.

It is important to understand that, although the nullity decree changes the status of the marriage in law, it does not actually make the marriage invalid. In the same way, a marriage certificate does not bring a marriage into existence but is simply the legal document that confirms the existence of the marriage in law. These are legal documents and it should be remembered that the law and reality do not always conform.

In the above definition of marriage nullity, the phrase "at the time of the wedding" is essential to that definition. The declaration of nullity refers back to the time of the wedding and effectively states that, although the law presumed that the marriage came into existence at that time, that presumption was false. Hence, a declaration of nullity amounts to a statement of fact. It reverses a legal presumption, but it does not change the fact. It is revealing a truth that was previously obscured by the law; that there was no marriage or, more precisely, that there was no marriage that the Church would recognise as such.

Sometimes, it is obvious that a marriage is invalid. However, even in that situation, remarriage is not possible until nullity has been formally declared. This might appear as a deprivation of the person's right to enter a true marriage. Yet, if people were allowed to make their own decisions about whether or not they had a valid marriage, there would be disorder in the life of the Church. The need for the Church to know the marital status of all people, not just Catholics, comes from a need in any society for order. Without control over the marital status of people, the Church might have difficulty in applying the teaching of Christ about permanence. It also seems right that the act of having a marriage declared invalid should have similar formality to the act of bringing a marriage into existence. Both have serious consequences for the couple and for the Church as a whole.

In order to discover how the Church approaches this question of nullity – that is, the question of whether or not a marriage exists in truth – it is necessary to understand how the Church determines the formation of a marriage. Canon law provides a definition of how a marriage is formed.

The law (canon 1057) states that a marriage is brought into existence by the lawfully manifested consent of people who are legally capable.

This statement contains three essential elements without which a marriage does not come into existence. If any one of these three elements is missing, a marriage, according to the Catholic Church, is potentially capable of being declared invalid. In summary form, these three elements are:

- <u>Consent</u>, which is the basis upon which a marriage is brought into existence; that is, each party agreeing to enter marriage with the other.
- This <u>consent</u> must be <u>lawfully manifested</u>; that is, given or expressed in a way determined by the law; for example, in a formal ceremony.
- That consent can be given only by people who are <u>legally capable</u>; in other words, people who in law are free to give consent to marriage.

These three essential elements are examined in detail in

the remaining chapters of this section.

Before proceeding, readers might be given a word of caution:
- To those in a stable marriage: remember that even if a marriage is technically invalid, the Church presumes that all marriages are valid. A long-lasting, wonderfully happy marriage can technically be invalid, but this does not prevent God bestowing upon it every blessing at His disposal. Hence, even if you think your marriage might be invalid, it is presumed valid. Ultimately, what is important is what God has united and not necessarily what is determined as valid by the Church's laws.
- To those who have suffered marriage breakdown, whether or not separated, please do not assume that you will obtain a declaration of marriage nullity because you have read something here that suggests your marriage may be invalid. A declaration of nullity of marriage is a serious matter and will only be granted when it has been proved with moral certainty that the marriage is invalid before the appropriate Church authorities.

Chapter 6

Lawful Manifestation

For any marriage to be recognised by lawful authority, whether that authority is the Church or the law of a particular country, consent to marriage must be manifested in a manner that the law determines. Hence, canon law sets down strict requirements that must be fulfilled if a wedding ceremony is to result in a marriage that the Church will recognise.

The manner in which consent must be exchanged is called the 'form' of marriage. Consent not manifested in the prescribed manner results in a marriage that can be declared invalid by reason of 'defect of form' or 'lack of form'.

It seems that some Catholics believe that any purely secular ceremony of marriage, for example, in a Register Office, hotel, beach or any other non-religious venue, is not recognised by the Church. This is not true. The Catholic Church will presume as valid any marriage, wherever it is celebrated, providing the parties gave consent in a manner in which the public perception was that they intended to form a marriage.

A Catholic, however, who does not marry in accordance with Catholic Church rules, marries invalidly, although it is still necessary for proof of invalidity to be produced to the relevant Church authorities before remarriage will be allowed.

For anyone who is baptised in the Catholic Church, canon law (canon 1108) states that marital consent must be exchanged before a person who is authorised by the Church; usually a bishop, a priest or a deacon but a layperson can also be authorised. That person is effectively the Church's witness to the formation of the marriage. The law is rather strict about which priest or deacon can receive the consent of the parties. For example, a parish priest usually has authority to conduct marriages in the parish to which he has been appointed as parish priest but a visiting priest may do so only with the permission of the parish priest or the bishop of the diocese.

There are various reasons that some Catholics do not approach the Church before celebrating their weddings. Some are unaware that the Church will recognise the marriage of its members only when certain conditions are met. Other Catholics marry in only a secular ceremony because of the presence of some impediment that means they cannot marry in a Catholic church. This might happen, for example, if a religious sister leaves her order to marry but does not wait until she has been released from her vow of chastity. Marriage in only a secular ceremony might occur if both parties were free to marry in secular law but not in canon law; for example, if one had been previously married. Other Catholics have simply lost their faith or have not been to church for so long that they would feel hypocritical marrying in a church.

There is much confusion and ignorance about this law of form and yet it can be easily understood if two things are remembered. The first is that some laws of the Catholic Church, those that are written by the Church purely for its own purposes (termed 'merely ecclesiastical'; that is, not of divine or natural origin), apply only to Catholics. This law of form is one such law.

This, then, means that the Church recognises as valid all marriages in which neither party is a Catholic. Thus, the marriage of two unbaptised people, who held their wedding ceremony before a secular registrar, would be recognised as valid by the Catholic Church, as would the marriage of a Baptist and an Anglican exchanging consent in an Anglican church, and the wedding of two Jews in a synagogue. Because none of these people are Catholics, they do not have to have a Catholic minister present when they exchange consent.

The second point to remember is that, for Catholics, it is not so much the place of marriage that is important but the presence of the official witness; the priest, deacon or delegated layperson who asks the parties to manifest their consent to one another and receives that consent on behalf of the Church. As merely ecclesiastical law, the law of form can be put aside if there is a good reason for doing so. Hence, a formal dispensation can be requested to enable the wedding to occur in a place other than a Catholic church. So, for example, a Catholic man might be granted a dispensation to marry in the Anglican church to which his intended wife has an affiliation.

So, barring some rare exceptions, it is possible to give simple guidelines for the application of this law of form when it comes to knowing if a wedding was validly celebrated. The rules may generally be summarised thus:
- It can be assumed that, if one or both of the spouses was Catholic and the wedding took place in a Catholic church, the marriage was validly celebrated. It may only have been celebrated elsewhere with the permission of the Church.
- It can be assumed that if neither spouse is Catholic the marriage was validly celebrated.

The purpose of this law of form is in part to safeguard the sanctity of marriage. The Church wants its members to recognise the gravity of the step they are taking in choosing marriage and so it encourages them to celebrate the wedding in a church, rather than in a more secular setting.

However, the law of form and its invalidating force does not fit easily into canon law as a whole and it can create some anomalous situations when marriage breakdown occurs. Consider, for example, the situation of a Catholic who has not practiced his faith for years and who, therefore, decides to marry his non-Catholic fiancée in only a secular ceremony. The marriage is reasonably happy for twenty years and produces three children. The couple then, for whatever reason, decide to separate and divorce. The man then meets a single Catholic for whom the faith is important and they decide to marry. Canon law would enable him to marry in a Catholic church, since he could easily have his first marriage declared null because of lack of form.

This is in sharp contrast to the situation that would have

prevailed had he married the first time in a Catholic church, or if he had not been a Catholic. In either of these two latter scenarios, it would have to be shown that his first marriage was invalid because of some other defect before he would be free to marry the second woman in the Church. Hence, in some circumstances, canon law can give the impression that the Church gives more favourable treatment to a Catholic who married outside the Church than to one who tried to follow the rules by marrying in a church.

From the spiritual viewpoint, too, this rule can give an impression that God will bless the marriages of those Catholics who marry in church, whilst withholding His grace from those Catholics who marry in only a secular ceremony. It is only fair to state that this is an unfortunate and unintended consequence of the law of form. Some reform of that law would appear useful, especially as the reason for its inception was a problem arising from clandestine marriage; a problem that hardly exists today.

Chapter 7

Legal Capability

Not everyone has the legal capacity to marry. Some are prevented from marrying by reason of a personal characteristic or status. If a marriage is to commence on the wedding day, both parties must have the freedom in law to marry at that time. In many countries, it would be rare for someone who did not have that freedom to be a party to a wedding ceremony. Those who are not legally free to marry are said to be impeded and the situation that prevents the person from having that freedom is called an impediment. Impediments to marriage are those things that the law specifically states will prevent a person from being capable of marriage. They may prevent marriage to every other person or they may prevent marriage to only some people.

Most impediments are public knowledge and so any proposed wedding would simply not be allowed. Usually, before a wedding occurs, both parties will have signed a declaration stating they are free from all impediments to the marriage. Even then, during the wedding ceremony and before they exchange consent, the bride and groom are usually asked to state publicly that they are not aware of any impediment to marriage and, often, everyone present is also asked to state if they know of any reason why the couple may not be joined in matrimony.

Many impediments in canon law are obvious, instantly recognisable and common to secular law. Some are peculiar to canon law or are not so familiar. Some impediments originate from divine or natural law and others contain elements that can be said to be of both divine and merely ecclesiastical origin. A bishop or his delegate can give permission, by use of a dispensation, to marry when the impediment is of ecclesiastical law alone. Naturally, when an impediment is of God's law, dispensation is not possible, except perhaps through the intervention of the Holy Father, using his position as Vicar of Christ.

The best way to understand canonical impediments is to explain each one. They are:

Age (canon 1083): A man may not marry before he is sixteen years old and a woman before she is fourteen years old. Most people would agree that natural law demands some minimum age for marriage. It has been known for girls as young as eight to become pregnant. Is this nature's way of saying they are approaching an age when they should be able to marry? The Church, anxious not to erect barriers that may frustrate the will of God, sets an age of fourteen years for girls and sixteen years for boys, even though people at those ages would normally be considered far too young to marry.

The actual ages of fourteen and sixteen are a matter of ecclesiastical law and, theoretically, permission can be granted for marriage at an earlier age. The age difference between genders would appear to give recognition to earlier development in maturity of girls.

<u>Impotence (canon 1084)</u>: the ability to have sexual intercourse is of vital importance to a marriage. It is the natural means by which procreation occurs. Within the context of a loving relationship, it is also a significant expression of the love of the spouses for one another and is the ultimate expression of the two becoming one. Hence, if a couple are unable to consummate their marriage because of a problem in either person, or even one that is relative to the couple – a problem of physical incompatibility – the marriage could be declared invalid.

Note that impotence, the inability to have intercourse, is not the same as sterility, which is an inability to conceive. Children are not certain in any marriage and sterility is not an impediment.

<u>Prior Marriage (canon 1085)</u>: this is perhaps the most obvious impediment to marriage. Since marriage is for life and the bond of marriage between two people continues until one of them dies, an impediment to another marriage always arises as soon as one marriage is celebrated. If the first marriage is later declared invalid, the legal impediment to another marriage lapses.

In reality, since a declaration of nullity is a statement that a marriage never began, it can be recognised that the impediment of prior marriage never existed in reality. The legal presumption of validity of a marriage causes also a presumption of an impediment to another marriage.

Non-baptism (canon 1086): the marriage of a Catholic to a person who is not baptised, assumed to be someone who does not believe in God, is considered to be potentially harmful to the faith of the Catholic. Hence, before such a marriage is allowed in the Church, the Catholic is asked to make various promises. These concern the upbringing of children and are intended to safeguard the faith of the Catholic. This impediment, from which a dispensation is usually granted, is known as the impediment of 'disparity of cult'.

Holy Orders (canon 1087): apart from married permanent deacons, the clergy of the Latin or Roman Catholic Church all make a promise of celibacy when they are ordained. Consequently, they then become impeded from entering marriage. This is a matter of merely ecclesiastical law and it could be changed at any time. The Eastern Catholic Churches have married clergy and we know that some of the apostles, who were the first bishops, were married.

If a priest or deacon should wish to marry, he is normally required to cease his ministry and apply to the Holy Father in Rome for a dispensation from all his clerical obligations, including that of celibacy. Once this is granted, he will be able to enter a marriage that the Church will recognise.

In more recent history, a significant number of married, former Anglican, male priests have been given permission to accept holy orders in the Catholic Church and thereafter to minister as Catholic priests whilst remaining married. This practice does not sit easily with the requirement that Catholic priests who wish to marry must leave their ministry. However, this is the current practice of the Church.

Religious Vows (canon 1088): anyone who has taken a

public, perpetual vow of chastity in a religious institute cannot validly enter marriage. The religious sister or brother must first seek permission and this would not be granted unless the person also applied to depart from the institute.

Abduction (canon 1089): a woman who has been abducted with a view to marriage and who remains captive is impeded from entering marriage. Only once she is freed, separated from her abductor and considered to be in a safe place is marriage possible. The law does not envisage a situation in which a man is abducted.

Murder (canon 1090): everyone consents to marriage 'till death do us part'. In order to discourage those who wish to remarry from murdering the first spouse so that remarriage can occur, the Church will not recognise the second marriage as valid. This impediment arises when either of the parties intending marriage has been party to the murder, either through their own hands or through a third party hired by either of them.

Blood Relationship (canon 1091): marriage is not possible between a person and his or her direct ancestors or descendants. So, a woman may not marry her father, grandfather, son or grandson. Marriage is similarly impossible between brothers and sisters. This is true even if they have only one parent in common. Special permission is needed to marry other close relations such as aunts, uncles, cousins and great aunts or uncles.

Relationship by Marriage (canon 1092): it is not possible to marry the natural parents or children of your deceased spouse. Thus, a man marries a widow, who has a daughter from her first husband. If the widow died, the man could not marry the daughter even though he is not naturally related to her. However, if the widow had a sister who was free to marry, there would be no reason why he and she could not marry.

<u>Public Propriety (canon 1093)</u>: when a man and a woman live together in a situation in which they are publicly perceived as having formed a common law marriage, they will be treated as though they had actually married should either of them later desire marriage to a relation of the other.

The impediment of public propriety would also arise from an invalid marriage. Hence, the impediment that would normally arise between two people because of the marriage of one to a relation of the other is considered to hold, even if that marriage is later declared invalid.

<u>Adoption (canon 1094)</u>: when a legal relationship is established by adoption, an impediment to marriage arises between the adopted person and the adopting parents and grandparents, and any natural children of those parents.

Most impediments would be known before marriage and so it is rare for any marriage to be declared invalid because of the presence of an impediment. Nevertheless, it is possible that awareness of some impediments might not occur until after a wedding, even after many years.

Chapter 8

Consent

It is usually easy to prove that a marriage is invalid because of lack of form or because of the presence of an impediment. The production of documentary evidence will normally be sufficient proof of many impediments. The impediments of murder and impotence might, however, be more difficult to prove. The impediment of murder, which would arise from the facts, whether or not the truth was known, might nevertheless require a successful criminal prosecution to prove the impediment. The impediment of impotence might be discovered only after the wedding.

Most applications for marriage nullity are processed under the general heading of a defect of consent. In the wedding ceremony, after announcing his or her intention to take the other, each says: "I take you to be my lawful wedded wife/husband." This is the moment of consent when each of the parties agrees to take the other as his or her spouse. This is the moment when the marriage begins.

In this act of consent, two things are presumed: that the intention of each spouse actually conforms to the words being said; and, that each is capable of giving valid consent to marriage. It is in showing that there was a serious defect of intention or a lack of capacity to give consent that a marriage can be declared invalid because of a defect in the consent of one or both of the parties.

How might this consent be defective? A story was printed in an English national daily newspaper some years ago of an American tourist who was visiting England for the first time. She had rented a car at the airport and driven off to enjoy her visit. After three days, she brought the car back to the airport complaining that it was too noisy, too slow and was consuming too much fuel. When a mechanic tried the car, he could find no fault with it. When he invited the woman to drive it again with him as a passenger, he discovered that she drove consistently in first gear. The woman had never driven a car with a manual gearbox and did not know how to use one. She had learned to drive in an automatic and had never driven anything else.

Before this experience, the woman would not have judged herself incapable of driving some cars. Before going to England, if asked if she could drive a car, she would have answered affirmatively. However, on returning to the States, she would probably have learned enough to qualify her response to such an enquiry. She had learned that her ability to drive was restricted to cars with automatic transmission. The point is that we all have limitations but we do not always recognise them.

We can all form relationships but many of us agree to form a marital relationship only once in our lives. No matter whether we have been prepared by the simple experience of having lived for a number of years or have set out deliberately to know and understand as far as possible what marriage will mean, actually entering into a marital relationship is a new experience that has the potential to be very different from expectations.

The decision to enter marriage is a decision for life. In order that two people do so validly, one of the requirements of canon law is that the parties have a basic understanding of what they are doing. Canon law (canon 1096) requires that the parties should not be ignorant that marriage is a permanent partnership between a man and a woman, and that it requires sexual cooperation to fulfil its purpose of the procreation of children.

This may appear very basic but it is possible that someone who has led a very sheltered upbringing may be unaware of how children are conceived. It is also possible for people to be ignorant of the nature of marriage as permanent, as a partnership of life or as requiring openness to having children. Note that this canon is concerned only with knowledge. Such knowledge would normally be presumed. Providing proof of ignorance of these matters would be hard, although not necessarily impossible.

Another ground for nullity arises when it can be shown that a person lacked sufficient use of reason (canon 1095 1°). This differs from the previous ground. In each situation, the person did not know what he or she was doing. However, under the first ground the person was simply ignorant of basic knowledge regarding marriage. The latter ground concerns the situation where a person gives consent whilst of unsound mind or whilst insane. In other words, the person is not able to understand the meaning or implication of the words said during the wedding ceremony.

It is the moment of consent that is important. Hence, a person might temporarily lack the use of reason, yet act rationally at most other times. If this person lacked sufficient use of reason at the moment of giving consent and this could be proved to the satisfaction of the Church, the marriage might be declared invalid.

What constitutes lack of use of reason might be a subject for debate. Many a father has stood in church and wondered if his daughter has lost her use of reason in her choice of marriage partner. This thinking, whilst of great concern to the father, would not be acceptable to the appropriate ecclesiastical authorities. The lack of objectivity in such an opinion would present something of a handicap to the required proof.

The Church is concerned that people entering marriage do so with good awareness of the commitment they are undertaking. Many things can deprive a person of sufficient use of reason. The man who had a few drinks before attending the church might have done enough damage to invalidate his consent if, for example, he is not aware of his actions. However, since lacking sufficient use of reason is such a vague phrase, the point at which a person's consent becomes invalid under the influence of alcohol would be difficult to determine. If it was suggested later that he lacked sufficient use of reason, there might be a presupposition that his behaviour at the wedding would be unreasonable; that is, that he did not treat the ceremony or those present with the respect and dignity that was deserved.

A person's use of reason could be affected by drugs, some temporary illness, fainting, delirium, an epileptic fit, or even excessive sleepiness. It should be said that, although these might render the person's consent invalid, they are more likely to prevent consent from being given at all, since the affected person will probably not be able to express the words of consent. The most likely outcome in most of these circumstances is that consent would be delayed until the person recovered from the temporary affliction.

Much more difficult situations, to which this ground for nullity is relevant, are those in which marriage is contemplated when one of the parties might be judged permanently to lack the use of reason. Who would be competent to make such a judgement? It would probably be unwise of anyone to attempt to do so.

Both of these grounds, whilst creating possibilities for declarations of nullity, are rarely examined as the reasons for which a marriage might be declared invalid. Amongst the more commonly examined grounds is that of 'lack of due discretion', or more properly expressed in the law as 'a grave lack of discretion of judgement concerning the essential matrimonial rights and obligations to be mutually given and accepted', which will now be examined.

Chapter 9

Grave Lack of Discretionary Judgement

From the earliest years of our lives, each of us makes many decisions every day that direct what we do, think and say. Many are simple and are made almost instantaneously and with little thought. Most are decisions we make very regularly and the consequences of making a poor decision are minor. Many require a little more consideration. All, at some time, will have involved an intricate process of thought, evaluation and judgement.

Take the decision to buy a pair of shoes. It consists of many elements, such as: do I shop on-line or visit a retail outlet, are the shoes the right colour, price, shape, style, fabric, size or comfort? Can I return them later if I decide I have made a mistake? If I have a deep social conscience, or have an interest in the shoe industry: where are they made, who by and using what materials? Similarly, the decision to eat in a restaurant involves decisions, such as distance to travel, taste, cost, recommendations, appetite and even mood.

These are just two examples that illustrate something of the complexity of thought and evaluative processes involved in making decisions. The more insignificant the decision, the less is the need to give time to considering, evaluating and judging the advantages, disadvantages and potential consequences of the decision. On a scale of important decisions in life, going to a restaurant or buying a pair of shoes would not rate as highly as, for example, deciding where to take a holiday or choosing a career.

For many people, the decision to marry would be very close to, if not at the top of the scale of important decisions. It is a decision with life-long consequences. It is not something that can be rectified easily if a mistake is made. It profoundly affects the lives of two people. As a decision with such grave consequences, the extent of thought, evaluation and judgement must be proportionately greater than that required for more mundane decisions. It stands to reason, therefore, that a person proposing to enter marriage should have a minimal knowledge of the nature of that covenant and the rights and obligations attached to it.

A man or a woman choosing marriage does so with one specific person in mind as the proposed spouse. Hence, consideration of matrimonial rights and obligations for a specific marriage will occur only with reference to a specific person. An important element in the giving of consent is some knowledge and awareness of the person to whom consent is given.

Canon law, then, recognises that the decision to form a marriage covenant with another person can be made only after some discernment. During this period of discernment, the decision regarding marriage can be broken down into smaller elements that might provide a focus for internal evaluation of the decision to marry or discussions with the proposed spouse. Each should consider carefully such matters as the nature of marriage as a life-long partnership requiring them to work together in every aspect of their lives, the requirement of fidelity and the matter of potentially having children and how they will be educated and nurtured. Each must also evaluate the state of their relationship and whether or not it can over time truly foster the well-being of both.

Put very simply, each potential spouse should have some knowledge of what is required to form a true marriage and have begun to picture himself or herself in that role of husband or wife to the intended spouse. Such a person would possess 'due discretionary judgement'. This ground for nullity (canon 1095 2°) is often referred to simply as 'lack of due discretion' or 'grave lack of discretion'.

Besides assessing the suitability of the other person as a potential marriage partner, due discretion of judgement requires by its nature a degree of self-perception and demands some self-knowledge and, by implication, an ability to make a realistic self-assessment. In other words, each must be able to judge, to some extent, his or her own fitness for the marriage covenant: the ability to be faithful, willingness to surrender a single-life mentality in favour of developing a partnership mentality and readiness to take on the responsibilities of becoming a parent, if that is to happen.

Most people who decide to marry would recognise these

things as a natural part of their decision. However, there are some people who remain gravely immature as adults or who have personality disorders such that it would be impossible for them to form a true marital relationship and there are others who simply don't know themselves well enough to make that judgement. Hence, if someone is conscious of a facet of personality that might seriously affect the ability to form a marital relationship, consideration of the potential effect of this should be part of the premarital evaluation process. It is, for example, well known that alcoholism can seriously affect a marriage. A person suffering from alcoholism who does not evaluate the effect of this addiction on a forthcoming marriage might give invalid consent on the wedding day.

What is required to obtain due discretionary judgement is nothing more than the natural process of evaluation before acting on any major decision.

A short courtship leading to marriage is never a good idea because of the limited time it allows for the parties to come to know one another. It is possible to form a successful marriage between two people who hardly know one another but the chances of future breakdown are surely increased. On the other hand, a long courtship does not bring with it a guarantee of successful marriage. Many couples now spend months or even years living together before marriage. Naturally, there are advantages to this in that the parties will come to know one another to perhaps a greater extent than if they had remained living apart. On the other hand, not all cohabitation without marriage provides a firm foundation for that later commitment. The extent of partnership of cohabiting couples will vary from couple to couple. Some will live very separate lives, while others will work very closely together. If cohabitation commenced before the couple entered a deeply committed relationship, behaviour patterns and the dynamics of their relationship may need to change if a marriage covenant is to be established. Cohabitation might commence between two people with entirely different expectations for the future. The woman might perceive it as an opportunity to deepen their relationship with a view to future commitment, whereas the man might see the arrangement as simply something that enhances his life and services his needs. Conversion from a cohabitation arrangement to successful marriage may not be straightforward. Failure to recognise that changes are needed to the dynamics of the relationship and/or to individual behaviour might indicate a grave lack of discretionary judgement.

It can happen that people set up home together and even have children together before there is any serious discussion concerning the future and their commitment to one another. Living in the present in this way, without due thought to the future and the effect on the people involved, most especially on the children and the possibility of them being raised in a stable and loving environment with both parents present, can give an appearance of immaturity and even irresponsibility. Some such parents later recognise the need to provide that environment and might attempt marriage when their relationship does not have the foundation to sustain it. Again, this could give rise to a claim of lack of discretionary judgement.

Hence, there is much that ought to be considered before two people are ready to commit themselves to one another in marriage. If there are different expectations concerning the future, for example, it is better to discuss these and find a compromise before making that commitment, because if there is no compromise then the marriage is likely to fail. If either has serious doubts about marriage, then it is better that these are discussed with someone, not necessarily the proposed spouse, rather than suppressed. If something is not right in the relationship before the marriage, it will not resolve itself simply because wedding vows are exchanged. If one does not love the other before marriage, such love may not grow during marriage. That annoying habit of hers before marriage is still going to be there during the marriage, unless she is informed and successfully manages to suppress it or he can learn to live with it. When a man in his late twenties still expects his mother to prepare his meals and do his laundry for him, his fiancée should be aware that he is likely to expect his mother or her to continue to do that even after they have married. It is not wise to defer these discussions until just before the wedding, because the pressure to continue is very significant once bookings are made, guests invited and everything else is arranged. Approaching marriage with the naïve mentality that difficulties will disappear after the wedding can indicate a grave lack of discretionary judgement.

Hence, discretionary judgement for marriage concerns mental processes: thoughts, evaluations and judgements that are made during the courtship period. There are many reasons why these processes might not occur and these will be considered when assessing if this ground for nullity is proved.

In any nullity application, the marriage was unsuccessful and it is appropriate to analyse why. An applicant might say he had serious doubts before the wedding. He and his fiancée always seemed to be arguing. They had met at work and got on so well that they decided to live together. There was no talk of marriage at that time but, two years later, she suggested they should marry. He didn't feel ready for that commitment but he didn't want to lose her and so he agreed to her suggestion. In his mind, they'd been happy till then and so why change things? She had said she wanted children but he had insisted they should wait until they were financially secure. He had left all the wedding plans to her, even though she had tried to involve him. On his stag night, he had become very drunk and told his best man he didn't want to do it. However, everything was arranged and he didn't feel able to back out now. Once married, he continued to live as though single. They had continued arguing and he found excuses not to be at home. The marriage soon failed. The man could be said to have been gravely lacking in discretionary judgement. His freedom to choose marriage was affected by his wish not to lose his partner. His approach to the marriage was strongly indicative of a grave lack in his judgement of the situation and its potential to produce an appropriate partnership of the whole of life.

When people are made aware of this ground of 'lack of due discretion', some ask: surely everyone can be said to have lacked discretion of judgement for marriage, for nobody knows fully what they are doing when they enter marriage? Marriage, after all, involves a life-time of discovery of the other person, the self and the commitment involved in the relationship.

This ground for nullity should not be taken out of context. It is true that nobody has perfect knowledge or understanding of the commitment they are undertaking. The law requires that a 'grave lack of discretion of judgement' should be proved before the ground can be cited as the reason for nullity.

Consider this example: a young couple in their late teens met at college and fell in love. It was the first experience of real romance for both of them. Despite having little in common, they felt grown up and enjoyed their new-found status. He put pressure on her for a sexual relationship and, rather than lose him, she reluctantly agreed. She was soon pregnant. Their parents were supportive but there wasn't really room at home for a baby and so they decided they would rent a flat and live together and he would find a job. He thought it would be better if they married and she agreed. She knew this would please her parents and so they quickly arranged the wedding. The marriage was not a success. After three years, she decided she had had enough. Problems had begun from the moment they set up house together, even before they married. He would come home from work, have his meal and then go out socialising with his friends. At first, he came home at a reasonable hour but, after the birth of their son, he started coming home later and often after drinking too much. His weekends were taken up with soccer. She tried to talk to him about her unhappiness but they would start arguing and he would storm off. Several times she discovered that he had spent the night at his parents' home rather than come home to her. Eventually, they separated and divorced. When she, a Catholic, decided she would want to remarry if she ever met the right man, she applied for a declaration that the marriage was invalid.

There are many aspects of this marriage that are relevant to the question of its validity. Discussion with the parties might elicit the following additional information:
- Both stated they married only because she was pregnant;
- Before the pregnancy, neither had given serious thought to the possibility that their relationship might end in marriage, even though she would admit that she hoped to marry one day;
- She had not envisaged marrying until she was at least in her mid-twenties; she wanted to finish her studies

and to develop a career first.
- He had thought of marriage only after she told him she was pregnant.
- After his first reaction of disbelief, he started to dream about his son as a future football star. The thought that the baby might be a girl did not cross his mind.

This information shows that her pregnancy had an obvious effect on the freedom of each in their decision to marry. She was influenced to marry by her awareness that to do so when pregnant would please her parents. He might admit that, in the circumstances, he wanted to be seen to do the right thing, which he interpreted as supporting her and, if necessary, marrying her. Each was concerned to do what was expected of him or her and it is likely that neither had given any serious thought to the future.

Furthermore, his behaviour once married would indicate that he was, at that time at least, unwilling and perhaps psychologically unable to make the required commitment. There seems to have been little perception of the requirement to form a community of life with his wife. His behaviour in staying out later and his excessive drinking after the birth of the child perhaps indicated an unwillingness to shoulder the responsibility of fatherhood, despite his good intentions at the time of the wedding.

The maturity of the parties would also come under scrutiny. Both were young at that time of critical decision-making. It was the first romantic relationship for each; a time when it might be difficult to distinguish infatuation from a genuine wish to seek the good of the other. The Church would take account of their youthfulness and might also attach some weight to this being the first romantic relationship for each.

A reflection of the maturity of each at that time is given in the information available. His fixation with his son as a future football star and virtual denial of the possibility that the child might be female is unrealistic. It is also relevant that she was perhaps more concerned about conforming with her parents' expectations than with making a decision that was right for her. This, too, might be perceived as a sign of immaturity.

These are just some of the conclusions that might be reached if this marriage was to be examined for invalidity. Care is being taken not to draw definitive conclusions. No marriage can definitely be said to be invalid, unless it is declared as such by competent authority. Nevertheless, there is a good chance that this marriage would be found to have been invalid.

This example might imply that all marriages to which consent was given on the occasion of a pregnancy can be interpreted as invalid. However, there is significant difference between a couple who marry only because she is pregnant and a couple who are preparing for marriage and then discover she is pregnant. The pressure in the first situation might be such that neither party appropriately evaluates the decision to marry, whereas the pregnancy in the second might cause only the date of the wedding to be brought forward but not have any effect at all on the desire for marriage. In the past, many couples found themselves marrying in such circumstances and there can be no doubt that many of these marriages have been happy and permanent. The validity of such successful marriages would never be questioned. It is important to realise that all things are possible to God.

It will be evident from all this that some maturity and depth of knowledge of life in general and marriage in particular is essential for a person to evaluate adequately the decision to marry, as is the need to carefully assess the potential for successful marriage with the specific intended spouse.

If a person is raised in a family in which marriage is seen as a disposable commodity, obtained lightly and put aside when no longer useful, it is likely that he or she would not evaluate marriage in terms of a permanent relationship that allows separation only as a last resort and without freedom to remarry.

The same can be said of anyone entering marriage with a gravely distorted view of any of the properties or essential elements of true marriage. For example, a man who as a boy became aware that his father was regularly unfaithful might not understand that such behaviour is not appropriate within marriage.

Lack of ability to perceive the situation in a realistic manner can occur for many reasons. For some, a first romantic encounter can be a traumatic and potentially bizarre experience. The first sudden realisation of reciprocated feelings for someone who finds you attractive, makes you feel important and special and says they actually like you, never mind love you, can turn the most sane and sensible person into an irrational and unreasonable wreck. That is perhaps an exaggeration but, for a while, being in the presence of, talking to, listening to or even just being in sight of the object of your infatuation can be the only thing on earth that matters. Under the influence of such overwhelming feelings, future marriage might be considered.

Fortunately, through the love-sick haze, most people can still grasp enough of reality to recognise this syndrome and only a very few will actually have married before the worst of these symptoms begin to subside. Returning to reality can be a great shock. In this state of obsession with another person, it is difficult to make rational and sensible decisions and those who do marry under the spell of infatuation may come to regret their decision.

However, it is not just infatuation that can induce a lack of realism. It is not uncommon for a person born to and reared by happily-married and contented parents to perceive marriage in terms only of that happiness. Such people may equate marriage only with peace, harmony and love and so have an overly idealistic view of marriage. Hence, there may be no recognition that a marital relationship can have its difficulties, become strained, that arguments can happen or serious tension can arise. Even when a proposed partner behaves badly during the courtship, the idealist may not be perturbed. She – for this seems to be a syndrome more common to women – fails to make an adequate evaluation of the reality of being married to that man. She often persuades herself that 'everything will be alright, once we are married'.

Mention has been made already of the need to make a realistic assessment of the effects of weaknesses of personality, such as alcoholism, before making a commitment of marriage. These weaknesses may naturally have an impact on the future married life. Thus, disabilities, whether of the mind or body, differences of faith or culture and/or unusual habits or traits of personality must form part of the process of evaluation before marriage. It is one thing to recognise a potential difficulty before marriage, but quite another to live with that difficulty twenty-four hours a day, every day.

This same reasoning is true for those who have

commitments that cannot be abandoned or put aside for the sake of the marriage. A person might have made a long-term commitment, for example, to the Armed Forces and could therefore be absent from the home for long periods. It would be necessary for the Armed Forces' member and any proposed spouse to evaluate the effect such commitment would have on their married life. Long absences are another factor that can result in breakdown of a marriage.

The pre-marital discussions of the couple would hopefully include not only how that commitment would be managed in the context of their marriage but also if it might continue into the future. The nature of marriage is such that, once married, additional commitment to the Forces after the expiry of the agreed term should not be made without consultation with the spouse. That commitment to the Forces had to be respected when the couple entered marriage. However, the nature of marriage means that any extension of the commitment should be made only as a joint decision of the spouses. However, even if the commitment is extended without consultation with the spouse, such an apparently selfish act would not necessarily have implications for the validity of the consent given at the time of the wedding.

When commitments to other people exist, these must also be taken into consideration in any decision to marry. Common to many couples choosing marriage is that one of them is already a parent and thus has responsibilities to one or more children. These may include full or part-time care, regular visiting, financial commitments and almost certainly some contact with a former partner or spouse. The approach of a parent to these responsibilities following the breakdown of the earlier relationship might be a useful indicator of the person's integrity and so of the qualities that he or she might be bringing into the intended marriage.

Anyone contemplating marriage who has care of another person would need to consider how the two commitments can be appropriately managed. The marriage partnership that is formed when two lives are joined together must embrace all that is necessarily part of those lives. Much will depend on the extent of dependency. When there is total dependency, such as a mother and young child from a previous relationship, there is a special need for careful evaluation.

Another situation that occurs, perhaps more commonly now than in the past, is when adults in later life agree to marry, perhaps when they have adult off-spring. The older years of the prospective spouses mean they will necessarily have more complex histories than those of a younger age. Adult off-spring may have several concerns about their father or mother remarrying. They may fear losing the parent or some particular gift that the parent offers, such as caring for grandchildren or providing financial support. They may be concerned about a potential future inheritance. They may see aspects of their parent's character that they have not seen before and may, possibly correctly, see the parents making an apparently foolish choice perhaps because of loneliness or ignorance.

When the matter is one of non-dependent off-spring, the parent who is seeking remarriage may feel forced to make a choice between the prospective spouse and the sons/daughters, if they disapprove or object. Ideally, of course, both the prospective spouse and the 'children' will celebrate the forming of an enlarged family and the happiness that this brings to the parent. However, this will not always occur. The nature of marriage, as a gift of the whole of life, demands that the prospective spouse should be put first once the marriage is celebrated. This might mean making difficult choices.

A future condition, that is a condition regarding the future attached to marital consent, is discussed in a later chapter. The tendency to want to protect family members is real. The notion that a wealthy mother might want to ensure her wealth is passed to her children, rather than to the relations of a prospective husband, is natural. Yet, this cannot be done in the form of a condition because such is contrary to the nature of marriage. It might be hoped that the husband, should he be the longer surviving spouse, would recognise some obligation to his former wife's children but such is not guaranteed. It is of the nature of these things that the future cannot be predicted and, to have due discretionary judgement, prospective spouses need only have duly evaluated those things that pertain to the forming at the time of the wedding of a partnership of the whole of life; giving and accepting the totality of two individual people. There can be no substitute for appropriate discussion of the potential difficulties that can arise and some acceptance that certain eventualities cannot be controlled. It may be that a decision not to attempt marriage might be appropriate.

It is useful to list typical examples of behaviour that might cause disturbance in a marriage and that might, therefore, indicate a failure to recognise the true nature of marriage. However, it must be remembered that this behaviour in itself does not cause a marriage to be invalid. These may be manifestations of a mentality contrary to the partnership aspect of marriage which might suggest there had been a lack of discretionary judgement. First the list, and then further discussion:
- Socialising without reference to the spouse.
- Selfishness with money or possessions.
- Making significant decisions without reference to the spouse.
- Turning to others rather than spouse when something

is not right.
- Inappropriate interaction with others; for example, flirtation or sexual advances.
- Unwillingness to discuss, compromise or see the partner's point of view.
- Selfishness in the sexual act.
- Failure to take a fair share of responsibilities; for example, household chores.
- Excessive time spent at work or in other activities that exclude the spouse.
- Unwillingness to have children or to share the responsibility of children.

Common to all of these, except perhaps the unwillingness to have children, is that they detract from the partnership aspect of marriage because they do not consider the needs of the spouse. In some marriages, certain elements of this behaviour will be quite acceptable and there will be no question of the behaviour creating marital tensions or leading to marriage breakdown. It may be that such behaviour is the result of a lack of discretionary judgement but it is unlikely that such lack would have been so grave as to have invalidated the consent of the person concerned.

It can be seen, then, that the joining together of two people in marriage constitutes the joining together of all that those people are and have. Pre-marital evaluation of the future partnership must necessarily include all that will be brought into that marriage.

In summary, if it can be shown that there was a serious failure to evaluate the marital decision, either in terms of the commitment involved or by reference to the circumstances of either party, and the marriage failed because of problems or difficulties that demonstrate that appropriate evaluation was not made, the marriage might be declared invalid.

The ground of lack of due discretion is a separate and distinct ground from that of inability, which is examined in the next chapter. Nevertheless, as will be seen, there is considerable overlap between the two.

Chapter 10

Inability

A simple principle forms the basis for this important ground for nullity. The principle can be stated as 'nobody is bound to the impossible'; in other words, if a person is not able to fulfil promises – in this case, the promises made on the wedding day – he or she can be said not to be bound by them. In legal terms, when the fulfilment of a contract is not possible, the contract can be declared null and void.

An example will demonstrate the principle. Before you pay me fifty million pounds to purchase a property from me, you are advised to ensure that I possess the title to that property and that I am legally able to pass it over to you. If I am not in possession of the title and I disappear with your money, you will have gained no better title to the property than you had previously. The contract will be invalid because it is impossible for me to pass over to you a title I do not possess.

Using similar reasoning, a marriage can be declared invalid if one of the parties is unable to assume one or more of the essential obligations of marriage (canon 1095 3°). That is, if it can be shown that, at the time of the wedding, one party could not, rather than did not, form that partnership of life and love that is marriage, the marriage will not have come into existence. What are the essential obligations of marriage? No official list of these exists but they can be discerned by reference to the purposes of marriage, which are the well-being of the couple and the procreation and education of children.

Hence, it is obvious that the ability to have sexual intercourse is an essential element of the marital relationship and not simply because intercourse is essential to the natural procreation of children. When intercourse is between two people who have made that gift of themselves to each other in a marriage covenant, it becomes a fundamental expression of the love of one spouse for the other. It is an act of love in its being other-centred; in other words, an act that, in its gift of self and acceptance of the gift of other, seeks both the well-being of the other as well as the self. When this physical expression of the gift of self is not possible at the time that consent is exchanged, the marriage might be declared invalid.

Some people believe that the non-consummation of a marriage means that the marriage is invalid. This is not true in Catholic canon law and the folly of such a notion becomes instantly apparent when it is recognised that the majority of marriages are not consummated for at least the first few hours of their existence. The marriage comes into existence at the moment of consent, not the moment of consummation.

However, it is possible that a non-consummated marriage might be declared invalid under this ground of 'inability', not because of the fact of non-consummation, but because of the reason for the lack of consummation.

Whereas the mere fact of non-consummation does not prove invalidity, it can be possible for parties to a non-consummated marriage to seek permission to remarry without obtaining a declaration of nullity. This makes use of the powers of the Holy Father to bind and to loose and is examined in Chapter 22.

Regarding those who are unable to assume the essential obligations of marriage, the law adds an element that might appear at first sight to create unnecessary difficulties. For invalidity to be declared using this ground, the law insists that the reason for the person being unable to assume the essential obligations of marriage must be founded in his or her psyche; that is, the inability must be for reasons of a psychological nature. Thus, this ground is not appropriate in situations in which the lack of consummation is due to physical problems. In such cases, the marriage might be invalid because of the presence of the impediment of impotence, provided that the problem existed at the time of the wedding.

If the problem was not present at the time of the wedding, the phrase 'for better, for worse' can take on its full and possibly onerous meaning. If a man had an accident that rendered him permanently paralysed so that full sexual relations were not possible, any marriage he might attempt could later be declared invalid because he would be unable to assume the essential obligations of marriage by reason of the impediment of impotence. However, if the wedding occurred before his accident, his later paralysis would be irrelevant to the validity or otherwise of the marriage.

The ground of 'inability' is concerned with those who are unable to assume the essential obligations of marriage because of causes of a psychological nature. However, it is not always possible to discern the precise reasons that a spouse did not honour marriage promises. Such failure might arise from an inability to do so, a simple unwillingness to adopt the role of spouse, or perhaps from a failure to evaluate the nature of the marriage covenant. A person contemplating marriage should have considered his or her ability to fulfil the marriage promises before exchanging consent on the wedding day. Thus, it can be argued that a person who was unable to fulfil the essential obligations of marriage, might also have been gravely lacking in discretionary judgement by failing to evaluate that inability, if the inability should have been known before the marriage. Thus, in many cases of inability it can be argued that the ground of lack of due discretion also applies.

In theory, of course, if everyone adhered to the moral code advocated by the Church, most people entering marriage would be inexperienced in sexual matters. As it takes time to develop other aspects of the relationship, so it takes time to develop the sexual element. Failure to consummate the marriage on the first night, or even within a few days or weeks, would not necessarily mean that the marriage is invalid. A temporary medical problem, for example, may mean that intercourse was unwise for a while. Embarrassment, initial tensions, fear of failure and general inexperience can lead to a very unsatisfactory sexual relationship in the early stages of marriage. Only if there is a lack of progress, such as no easing of embarrassment or tension or confidence waning rather than growing, might there be grounds for nullity.

Over time, the Church has come to accept that a single act

of intercourse or even rarely occurring acts, although consummating a marriage, would not be sufficient to prevent a declaration of nullity because of the existence of a sexual problem. Each person must have the ability, at the time of consent, to make a gift of self over an extended period of time. Thus, it is to be expected that each couple would reach some acceptable level of sexual intimacy during the course of the marriage. Failure to do so might indicate an inability to make an appropriate gift of self and so be the foundation for a plea of nullity.

The success or otherwise of the sexual relationship within marriage can be a useful indicator of the success or otherwise of the marital relationship as a whole and so a temporary or lasting lack of sexual relationship within marriage might have no implications for nullity. Implications for nullity will usually arise only when a problem has existed since the wedding day.

The importance of the sexual relationship within marriage means there are many areas of concern when it comes to a consideration of validity. It is not just the absence of a sexual relationship that might be important. Any acts that might be said to place a greater emphasis on self-gratification rather than pleasing the other or something for the good of both parties, might be relevant when it comes to challenging the validity of a marriage. Such acts might imply a lack of understanding of the self-giving or partnership aspect of marriage and hence lead to questions regarding the discretionary judgement of the person. This might occur, for example, when one party demands the use of unusual or unnatural practices.

The sexual relationship in marriage should be primarily an act of love, comprising a gift of self and embracing the well-being of the other. Sexual practices that have these as their end would not be invalidating. The Church would be more concerned about practices that gave pleasure to one spouse but were abhorrent to the other, or practices that strike at the very heart of marriage; for example, swapping partners with another couple for mere sexual gratification. It will be clear that a practice that gives pleasure and joy to one couple might be totally abhorrent to another. It is only insofar as any practice seriously detracts from a particular marriage covenant that there might be implications for nullity.

Homosexuality and lesbianism can also present reasons for nullity using this ground. Marriage has always been understood by the Church as the joining together of a man and a woman. Same sex unions, even if having value in themselves, are not recognised as marriages by canon law or by wider Church teaching. Hence, the ability to give oneself in marriage as recognised by the Church implies a basic heterosexual orientation; in other words, an ability to give oneself in heterosexual acts over an extended period of time. Difficulties can arise in determining the correct use of this ground in situations when there appears to be latent homosexuality or bisexuality. Determining when a person's sexual orientation or practices might constitute grounds for nullity is rarely a simple matter. For example, occasional homosexual acts by a married man would not necessarily prove invalidity using this ground. Yet, any sexual act that does not include the spouse, such as use of pornography, masturbation or even flirting, might be deemed by the other as an act of betrayal or infidelity.

The general principle for this ground of nullity is that each party should be capable of acting in a manner compatible with the nature of marriage. Hence, there are implications for nullity when either party consistently behaves in any manner that might be contrary to the nature of marriage as a partnership of the whole of life seeking the well-being of the spouses.

Aggression in any form or any type of behaviour that consistently undermines the well-being of the spouse might form the basis of a claim of nullity under this ground. Examples of such behaviour might be: persistent swearing, belittling the beliefs of another, speaking about or behaving badly towards people loved by the other, silent treatment, refusal to communicate in a respectful manner, name-calling, constant criticism, threatening physical or emotional harm, refusal to recognise or celebrate achievements, persistent sarcasm, regular criminal activity, gross mismanagement of finances, refusing to apologise, deprivation of human essentials, or bullying behaviour. In short, any consistent behaviour that does not respect the dignity of the spouse or that might be termed abusive can be cited as evidence that might prove this ground.

There is a danger, however, that every element of inappropriate behaviour might be interpreted as invalidating. Nobody is perfect. Everyone brings human flaws into his or her marriage. For example, it might be argued by the woman of an unfaithful husband that his infidelity amounted to acting in a manner that detracted from the true nature of their marriage. This might be a true interpretation of his actions but, to prove invalidity on the ground that he was unable to assume the essential obligations of marriage, it would be necessary to show that his infidelity resulted from a personality disorder and was not simply a moment of weakness or sin; in other words, that he could not really help himself. Persistent acts of destructive behaviour might prove this ground but isolated failings might not.

The conditions, known as nymphomania for women and satyriasis for men, amount to having an abnormally high sex drive and can mean that the person is unable to remain faithful in marriage. The existence of such a condition would normally be manifested by a history of infidelity with different partners. However, infidelity in marriage, even with several different partners, could be a sign of many different things and the specific conditions of satyriasis and nymphomania cannot be assumed. Besides the possibility that such an act might have been a moment of weakness or sin, infidelity could also be an indication of an unhappy marriage, of a selfish personality or of ignorance of the nature of marriage. The breach of trust that arises from infidelity usually causes significant damage to a marriage and so the Church would always consider if such acts might be relevant to the validity of the consent given on the wedding day. Nevertheless, establishing a link between such acts and that consent can be difficult and it might be concluded that such a link either was extremely unlikely or did not exist at all.

Like many grounds for nullity, then, it is the facts of the marriage that determine if the ground of inability is appropriate in a particular case. Any personality disorder, which by definition is grounded in the psyche, can be invalidating if it results in a union that seriously undermines the well-being of either spouse or that of the children. The same is true of certain mental illnesses, dependencies such as alcohol or drug addiction, or even a more temporary debilitating condition such as bereavement. The Church will examine each case on its merits. It is obvious that the minor imperfections present in everyone's personality would not in themselves mean that a marriage is invalid. There is always an important distinction to be made between circumstances that render a marriage invalid and those that simply make it difficult. The latter would not of themselves provide grounds for nullity.

Invalidity does not always result from the obvious manifestations of a problem but from some less obvious cause. A man who drinks heavily and who becomes dependent on drink during the marriage might have started drinking as an escape from, say, the responsibilities of fatherhood. Since the procreation and education of children is one of the ends of marriage, a partner who is unable to accept parental responsibilities could be judged unable to assume the essential obligations of marriage, providing that inability was the result of a problem existing at the time of the wedding. In this example, it would be the inability to accept the responsibilities of parenthood that would render the marriage invalid, rather than the problem with alcohol.

The variety and type of problems that might come under the umbrella of the ground of inability is virtually limitless. A consistent threat to a marriage might arise from one serious difficulty or a combination of minor problems.

It is also apparent that the behaviour or personalities of two people might make marriage between them impossible, yet each would be capable of successful marriage with others. For example, two fiery-tempered and stubborn individuals might find marriage to one another impossible since the smallest argument would result in a complete breakdown of communication with little hope of reconciliation. Yet the marriage of one of these to a more placid and forgiving person might lead only to short-lived and soon forgotten arguments.

Parental behaviour towards children can also provide a reason to allege that a marriage is invalid using this ground. One of the ends of marriage is the procreation and education of children. Hence, any form of serious abuse of children of the marriage by a parent might lead to an allegation of nullity. Again, however, there is a need to recognise that the perfect parent does not exist and this ground concerns those who are unable to assume the essential obligations of marriage, not those who simply could have or should have done better.

The use of this ground of inability in the marriage nullity process relies very much on the principle of 'the proof of the pudding is in the eating'. Whilst it can be very difficult to claim that one of the parties was unable to assume the essential obligations of marriage when that marriage had survived over many years, there is a need to discern the difference between a couple struggling with a successful marriage and a couple who have simply resorted to living together when the marriage has all but failed.

Chapter 11

Error and Fraud

There are two more grounds for marriage nullity that might come under the general heading of those who are unable to give valid consent. They concern the areas of error and fraud. Although the scope for the use of these grounds is limited, they are occasionally cited as the grounds for declaring a marriage invalid.

Error arises from within the erring person when he or she has drawn an incorrect inference or conclusion about something. The cause of the error might be simple ignorance. It could also arise from an act of fraud; that is, the error occurs because a deliberate action by another person is taken to ensure that an incorrect inference or conclusion is drawn. Thus, I am in error if I marry a woman whom I believe to be rich, when she is in fact penniless. There is fraud attached only if she, or somebody else, has taken steps to lead me to believe she is rich; or, knowing that I believe she is rich, she has made no attempt to correct me. Needless to say, the error has to be significant to justify a claim that the marriage is invalid. It has to be an error that strikes at the heart of the marital undertaking.

Error of person invalidates a marriage (canon 1097 §1). If my intention is to marry one woman, and the bride lifts her veil at the end of the ceremony to reveal a different woman, the marriage can be declared invalid. I made a mistake by giving my consent to the wrong person. I can therefore claim that my consent was invalid.

Much more likely is that an error will concern a quality of a person; that is, the error relates to some element of the person's character or physical being. The possibility of the marriage then being declared null depends upon whether or not that quality was directly and principally intended (canon 1097 §2). This can be better understood by recognising that a quality that is directly and principally intended cannot effectively be distinguished, in the mind of the other, from the person who has that quality. Thus, the quality is so important to the marrying partner that the marriage would not be taking place without it; in other words, in the mind of the marrying partner, the quality and the person are synonymous. In practice, the test here is the effect on the marriage of the truth being discovered. In other words, I cannot claim that a quality was directly and principally intended if my discovery that the quality does not exist has little effect on my desire to remain in the marriage.

Hence, if a woman of strong Catholic faith decides she wants to marry a man who shares that faith, she might claim her marriage is invalid if she finds after the wedding that he husband does not believe in God.

Other examples that might provide opportunities for the use of this ground could be such qualities as paternity, serious disease or illness, a professional qualification, guilt of a serious crime or virginity. In investigating claims that the marriage was null, the Church would expect to hear statements such as: "I thought she was carrying my child and that was why I married her"; "I would never have married him if I had known he was HIV positive"; or "I would never have married him if I had known he was guilty of that crime".

The range of possibilities for the use of this ground is extensive. However, in practice it is very difficult to show that a quality was so fundamental to the decision to marry that, without it, the marriage would not have taken place. Marriage is, after all, the joining together of two people, which is more than the joining together of two sets of qualities. It is for this reason that only the lack of a quality that is principally and directly intended will invalidate. Any other quality is incidental to the essence of the marriage.

The ground of fraud is similar to that of error. If the fraud is such as to secure the consent of the other, the marriage can be declared invalid, but only if the fraud was of such a nature that it could seriously disrupt the partnership of conjugal life. Note, the law says it is the person who was defrauded who gives invalid consent (canon 1098), not the perpetrator of the deceit. Indeed, the perpetrator of the deceit does not have to be the other party to the marriage. It might be a relation or friend who wants the wedding to take place. Again, what is important to prove invalidity is that the person subject to the fraud is in serious error about the person he or she is marrying.

Fraud that might cause consent to be invalid has to be grave. It has to have been perpetrated to secure the consent of the other. If a man makes it known to his girlfriend that he is only willing to marry a virgin, and she hides from him the fact that she is not, he is entitled to claim invalidity.

Error and fraud can also give rise to circumstances that might be relevant to other grounds for nullity. For example, if I am determined to marry only a practicing Christian but do not question my intended spouse on this subject before marriage, it might be claimed that my discretionary judgement was lacking. Remember, however, that it takes a grave lack of discretionary judgement to invalidate a marriage.

The implications for other grounds are much more serious for fraud than for error, assuming the fraud is perpetrated by the other spouse. Any deception, but especially one so grave that it was intended to secure consent, is potentially damaging of the marital relationship, the good of which is very largely dependent on mutual trust. The discretionary judgement of anyone, therefore, who is prepared to deceive the other to that extent, must be in doubt, since it has grave implications for that person's understanding of marriage. It is difficult to reconcile such deception with the essential gift of self that marriage demands.

Chapter 12

Defects of Intention

Grounds for nullity also arise when there is a serious defect in the intention of one of the parties at the time of the wedding (canon 1101). These defects of intention amount to 'simulation'. Those who simulate their consent are saying one thing with their lips but intending another in their hearts. Effectively, the words they speak at the moment of consent are a lie.

When the parties say the words of consent, it is presumed that they mean what they say and interpret those words in the same way as they are generally understood. However, this does not always happen. Simulation is 'total' when marriage itself is excluded from the intention of the simulating person, or it is 'partial' when marriage is intended but some element such as fidelity, children, permanence or the good of the spouses is excluded.

Total simulation would occur, for example, when two people perform a wedding ceremony simply so that one can acquire a new civilian status. If a person entered the country on a student visa and wished to stay at the end of his studies but could not obtain an extension to that visa, marrying a person from the host country might result in a right to residence. Of course, it is often a breach of secular law to marry simply to gain nationality. Despite this, the Church would still require that a declaration of nullity was granted before either party could marry again.

The more obvious cases of total simulation are identified by the brevity of the time the spouses live together after the wedding. In some cases, cohabitation never occurs. The 'spouses' simply come together for the wedding ceremony and then go their separate ways. Nevertheless, the Church also recognises that total simulation can have occurred even in a situation in which the spouses have spent many years together. One proof of total simulation is in showing that there was some motive for the simulator to give consent to marriage without actually intending to form a marriage.

The mere presence of a motive is never proof that simulation actually occurred. A man might consent to marry a woman because she is very rich and he wants access to her money for his own purposes. If he had no intention to establish with her a partnership of life, he can be said to have simulated his consent, for what was in his heart on the wedding day was her money and not any intention to establish with her that partnership of life that is true marriage. If, however, her wealth was only an incentive for him to choose her as his wife and his intention was nevertheless to make a gift of himself to her in marriage, simulation will not have occurred.

The documents of the Second Vatican Council teach that a true marriage arises from a community of the whole of life of the spouses. The spouses can be said to have a right to this community of life and so people who marry but do not order their lives in such a way as to allow the formation of that community of life may have simulated their consent.

Of course, there can be separation that does not arise from the simulation of one of the parties. This might happen, for example, at a time of war when the parties might be separated very soon after the wedding and for a long period of time but the intention of each would be to form a community of life as soon as that was possible.

Simulation might also occur without physical separation. A married couple can live in the same house but live such separate lives that a community of life is absent. Some typical manifestations of the denial of the right to a community of life might be: a refusal to socialise with the other, a refusal to share finances, a refusal to mix with the family and friends of the spouse, failing to take an interest in the spouse's work, taking separate holidays, putting the needs of others before those of the spouse, seeking only self-satisfaction in the sexual act and a refusal to hear or discuss the concerns of the other.

Some of these manifestations of lack of partnership are not necessarily proof of an intention against marriage. If such an intention really existed, it would be expected that these aspects of behaviour would be present from the beginning of the marriage. Much more likely is that only some of these signs are present, in which case it might successfully be argued that there was a distorted or false perception of the meaning of marriage, rather than a rejection of marriage itself. The lack of any one or more of these in a particular marriage might also simply be a sign of lack of perfection in that marriage, rather than proof of invalidity.

The other grounds for nullity that might be proved under this general heading of simulation concern the rejection of only a particular but essential aspect of marriage. One of the more frequently examined of these grounds concerns an intention by one or both parties to exclude children from their marriage. Since one of the recognised purposes of marriage is to provide a stable environment in which children might be raised, a marriage in which one of the parties is determined not to have children is not a marriage as understood by the Church. Nevertheless, many good marriages are naturally childless and others do not result in children for many different reasons. Hence, in any case in which an intention against children is alleged, great care is needed in interpreting the facts.

Marriage involves the exchange of certain rights. One right recognised by the Church is the right to sexual acts that are generative of children. Note, there is no right to children in a marriage. The right is only to those acts that can result in pregnancy. Insofar as that right is denied, the marriage covenant is not being fulfilled.

Even until relatively recently, this right to acts generative of children was interpreted by some secular courts as meaning that rape between persons who are married was not possible. Now, however, it is recognised that the rights proper to marriage include each spouse's right to respect and dignity; a right that takes precedence over any right to sexual relations.

There is an important distinction to be made between the denial of rights and the choice not to use those rights. Many couples who marry choose to delay starting a family. The right to procreative acts generative of children is only denied when one of them consistently frustrates the wishes of the other to have children. Such denial must always refer back to the start of the marriage to prove nullity. A denial that begins after a few years of marriage is not in itself invalidating. Recognising that a marital relationship has become unhappy or unstable can result in a decision, even a unilateral decision, to avoid bringing children into that situation.

The matter is potentially quite difficult because, besides partial simulation, the denial of the right to sexual acts generative of children might suggest other grounds for nullity. For example, a man who simply does not want the responsibility of fatherhood might have failed to make a proper evaluation of the nature of marriage. The same might be said if either party saw the furtherance of a career, individual interests or three overseas holidays a year as a higher priority than having children. A woman might refuse to have children because of fear of the pain of childbirth and so might be deemed unable to assume the essential obligations of marriage. This is not to say that a marriage involving any of these people could not be happy and apparently blessed by God. However, should any of them fail there might be grounds for declaring such marriages to have been invalid.

Partial simulation can also occur when one of the parties does not recognise or accept that what is being undertaken is a permanent commitment. This would occur when one party reserved the right to end the marriage at will and so considered himself or herself free to enter a new marriage. Again, care is needed. Is it possible to distinguish a genuine intention at the time of the wedding to end the marriage at will, from the reality that seeking divorce through the secular courts can bring practical benefits once a marital relationship has resulted in permanent separation? Even those with fervent belief in the permanence of marriage may seek a secular divorce when his or her marriage has irretrievably broken down, because of the practical benefits of doing so. Although there may be exceptions, this act at the time of separation cannot normally be said to have implications for the validity of consent given at the start of the marriage.

More and more people are insisting on a pre-nuptial agreement being signed before they will commit themselves in marriage. A pre-nuptial agreement is usually an agreement that determines ownership of certain assets if the marriage fails. It might protect a wealthy person from losing a substantial part of that wealth when a marriage is short-lived. However, it can even be used, for example, to protect ownership of a treasured possession such as a family heirloom or even a much-loved dog.

In any application for a declaration of nullity of marriage, the presence of a pre-nuptial agreement might be taken by the Church as a sign of an intention against the permanence of marriage. It might be proof of a divorce mentality, since it appears that future breakdown of the marriage is anticipated. However, not all pre-nuptial agreements are written in the belief that the marriage will not last and it is possible to envisage a situation in which such an agreement is written, say, to safeguard the future inheritance of children from a previous union in the event that the marriage fails. The presence of a pre-nuptial agreement can have implications for some possible grounds for nullity, or for none.

There would also be partial simulation if the element of fidelity in marriage was excluded from the consent of one of the parties. This would occur when the person was open to the possibility of having sexual relations with others, if the opportunity arose.

Of course, it would be difficult to prove such an intention. An act of adultery is much more likely to occur because of a moment of weakness, perhaps when a marriage is having difficulties, than because one of the spouses considers fidelity in marriage to be unimportant. However, a plea of intention against fidelity might be successful if it was shown that there was a continuing inappropriate relationship with another person at the time of the wedding, or there was a pattern of regular infidelity throughout the marriage.

Again, another ground, rather than a defect of intention, might be more appropriate when regular infidelity is alleged, as such can be a sign of a poorly evaluated decision to marry or a personality disorder. In which cases, the grounds of lack of due discretion or inability could be more appropriate.

It will be obvious from all that has been said about defects of intention that a reliable confession from the simulating party would make proof of these grounds of total and partial simulation quite simple. However, proof can also be possible when a verbal or written confession is not forthcoming. Indeed, the Church recognises that the deeds of the simulating party during the marriage can often speak more effectively than any words of confession.

Chapter 13

Other Defects of Consent

This section would not be complete without an examination of other possible grounds for nullity that can arise from a defect of consent. In practice, however, the number of cases in which they might be used successfully is limited.

The essence of marriage is an unreserved gift of one spouse to the other. Hence, the law has something to say if one or both parties attempt to impose conditions on consent because such conditions almost invariably amount to a reservation of the gift of self. The very nature of a condition means that the marriage would not otherwise occur. If the man tried to impose a condition on the woman that she refused to accept and they nevertheless married, it would be very difficult to claim that he gave conditional consent.

The law (canon 1102) states that a marriage cannot be contracted validly if one of the spouses imposes a condition concerning any aspect of their future life as a married couple. Some possible examples of invalidating conditions might be:
- "I will marry you only if you bear me a male heir."
- "I will marry you only if my mother can also live with us."
- "I will marry you only on condition that you never drink alcohol again."
- "I will marry you only on the condition that if the marriage fails you will be entitled to no more than one million pounds of my fortune."

It is, however, possible to enter a valid marriage when a condition is imposed that concerns the past or present. The following conditions would, therefore, be possible:
- "I will marry you only on condition that you are a millionairess."
- "I will marry you only on the condition that I am the father of the child you are carrying."
- "I will marry you only on the condition that you are not guilty of the crime with which you have been charged."
- "I will marry you only on the condition that you are a virgin."

The validity of the marriage will depend on the condition being satisfied at the time of exchanging consent. If the past or present condition is not satisfied, the marriage is not valid. However, nothing changes if the millionairess loses half her fortune in a stock market crash the day after the wedding, for once valid consent is given it cannot be revoked. As long as she was a millionairess at the time of exchanging consent, the marriage is valid. If it was later shown that the condition was not satisfied at the time of the wedding, the marriage can be declared invalid.

The final ground under the general heading of defect of consent concerns force and fear (canon 1103); there are others concerning marriage by proxy that will not be discussed here. The ground of force and fear concerns those for whom marriage is seen as their only option when under the influence of some force or grave fear inflicted from outside, such as a threat of physical harm should the wedding not take place.

This situation should be distinguished from those who perceive marriage as their only option because of a set of circumstances, such as the girl being pregnant. In these situations, people are usually reacting to a moral or social obligation – some interior prompting – rather than from a sense of fear of some external reprisal that will occur if they don't marry. The ground of force or fear would not apply in such circumstances, unless there was some outside agent, such as the girl's father, threatening to kill the boy if he did not marry her. However, it suffices for the boy to believe that the father will kill him, even if the father would not actually do so.

It stands to reason that this ground will apply only when one or both parties would not have entered marriage but for that force or grave fear. For example, a woman might continue with an engagement because her fiancé has threatened to kill himself when she mentioned wanting to break it off. Of course, such circumstances could also give rise to other grounds for nullity. Such emotional blackmail is not compatible with the nature of marriage.

One additional aspect of this ground is worth mentioning.

The Church's jurisprudence has come to recognise what is described as 'reverential fear'; that is, fear that can arise from a relationship of dependency such that, if a prescribed outcome such as marriage does not occur, it is feared that the relationship might be irreparably damaged. This relationship might be familial but it could also arise in any situation in which a figure of authority is held in such reverence that the person finds it impossible to make a decision independently of the authority figure.

Enough has been said about the theory of marriage nullity. The next section explains how a person applies for a declaration of marriage nullity and how such an application is processed. There are ways other than nullity in which it is possible for some to enter another union that the Church will recognise as a valid marriage and these will be examined in the final section.

SECTION II

Chapter 14

The Tribunal System

Until now, use of the word 'tribunal' has been avoided. It is a word that has many connotations and it might conjure up images that could deter some from making an application for a declaration of marriage nullity. The reality, however, is that an investigation into a marriage for possible invalidity is conducted using judicial processes by a diocesan tribunal, which is effectively a Church court.

Before 2015, applications for marriage nullity were processed using either a documentary procedure or a formal judicial procedure. In 2015, Pope Francis introduced a briefer but still judicial process that can be used if particular circumstances exist.

A documentary process is usually appropriate when invalidity is alleged either by reason of a defect of form or by the presence of an impediment. As its name suggests, proof of invalidity comes from producing the relevant documents that demonstrate, for example, that one of the parties in a secular ceremony of marriage was a Catholic at the time of the wedding. Similarly, many impediments can be proved by producing documents.

Applications for nullity that cannot easily be proved using the documentary process, and this would include all cases in which invalid consent is alleged, would be subjected to a formal judicial process.

Each diocese should have its own tribunal. The tribunal is headed by the diocesan bishop. However, canon law requires the bishop to appoint an 'Officialis' or 'Judicial Vicar', whose role is to manage the tribunal and its case load. The tribunal will also have other personnel appointed to undertake particular functions in the judicial process.

The function of the tribunal is usually defined by the diocesan bishop and it can be asked to judge on any matters of contention within the diocese. However, tribunals rarely handle contentious matters other than applications for a declaration of nullity of marriage. For this reason, many diocesan tribunals have become known simply as marriage tribunals.

Some bishops do not have a sufficient number of qualified personnel or other resources to enable the establishment of a diocesan tribunal. When this happens, two or more dioceses may share a tribunal and these are known as inter-diocesan or regional tribunals. The whole of Scotland, for example, is served by one tribunal. Ireland is served by four regional tribunals.

Besides these tribunals, the role of which is to hear cases in first instance, there is a system of appeal tribunals, also known as tribunals of second instance. These are tribunals designated by the authorities in Rome to hear appeals against the decisions of the first instance tribunals. In England and Wales, for example, the tribunals of the Westminster, Liverpool, Southwark and Birmingham Archdioceses have been appointed as appeal tribunals. In Ireland, a separate tribunal has been established to hear appeals from the regional tribunals.

Besides this second level of tribunals, there is the Roman Rota. This is the usual third instance tribunal and it hears appeals from appeal tribunals. However, the Rota can also hear any case, from anywhere in the world, in first, second or third instance.

Finally, certain cases, such as those involving Heads of State, are specifically reserved to the Holy Father, through the Rota. The purpose of this is to ensure that local tribunals can act without any undue influence from secular powers. This may appear to be granting special privileges to the rich and famous but, in reality, the Rota is likely to take longer to complete the application than many local tribunals.

Since the changes introduced by Pope Francis is 2015, applications for nullity using the formal process can result in a decree of nullity being issued after only one hearing, providing no appeal is lodged against the tribunal's decision. Before December 2015, every judgement in favour of nullity in first instance had to be passed to an appeal tribunal for a review and ratification of that decision before a decree of nullity could be issued.

The first step in any application for nullity is for one of the parties to the marriage to contact a tribunal and request an investigation into the marriage. Except in very rare cases. the only people who can apply for nullity of a marriage are the spouses; either one of them, or both together.

Tribunals can accept cases for hearing only if they have competence in relation to the particular case. The rules on competence were also changed by Pope Francis in 2015 and now provide applicants with more tribunals to which they can apply for nullity. A tribunal is competent to hear a case if: the applicant lives in the diocese served by the tribunal; the other spouse lives in the diocese served by the tribunal; the wedding was celebrated in the diocese served by the tribunal; or, most of the evidence will be gathered in the diocese served by the tribunal. Hence, upon receiving an application for nullity, the tribunal has first to determine if it is competent to hear the case. A tribunal that is not competent will usually pass the case to one that is competent.

Once a case is accepted for hearing, it should be assigned to one particular person within the tribunal who will take responsibility for instructing the case. This is usually one of the judges. It is the responsibility of the instructing judge to ensure that the rights of the parties are respected and that all appropriate evidence is collected. The instructing judge should carefully monitor the case from start to finish. The duties of this judge will include drawing up special questions to take account of the particular circumstances of the case, ensuring that appropriate grounds are examined, ensuring that the parties are kept properly informed and ensuring that the case is not unduly delayed in its progress to completion.

Before closing this chapter, it is worth offering a word of comfort for those deterred by the thought of approaching a 'tribunal'. The parties are never asked to present themselves before a panel of tribunal personnel or to attend a formal court hearing. It seems that some people are deterred by the thought of having to admit that they have remarried outside the Church, that they were unfaithful in the marriage or that they behaved in some other way that might be thought to show them in a bad light. Tribunal personnel are used to hearing such confessions and it is not their function to make moral judgements. As a part of the Church, the tribunal shares its mission of the salvation of souls. The work of the tribunal, although by nature juridical, is primarily pastoral and largely confidential.

Chapter 15

The Petitioner

The petitioner is the person who applies for a declaration of nullity of the marriage. In theory, the application begins by the person presenting a petition to the diocesan bishop asking for an investigation into the validity of the marriage. In practice, however, very few petitioners approach the tribunal in this manner. Most contact the tribunal through a third party, such as their parish priest. However, the contact details for most diocesan tribunals can be found on the relevant diocesan website and potential applicants can contact the tribunal directly and are encouraged to do so.

Any person, whether Catholic or non-Catholic, can apply for a Catholic declaration of nullity of his or her marriage as long as the other party to the marriage is still alive. A person who is not a Catholic might want to apply in order to be declared free to marry a Catholic or might be in a second marriage and contemplating asking for reception into the Church. Most of the requirements for valid consent are of natural law and so apply to all people, whatever their faith. Hence, the Church freely assumes competence to judge the validity of marriages even when neither party is Catholic, as long as one of the spouses applies and there are sound pastoral reasons for the tribunal to accept the case for hearing.

The usual reasons for presenting a nullity application are that the petitioner wants to remarry, or has already married in a secular ceremony and wants the second union recognised by the Church. Another common reason for applying seems to be that the petitioner wants to gain some peace of mind from a successful application.

The first duty of the tribunal is always to safeguard the sanctity of marriage by ensuring that, if there is any hope of success, the couple are given every opportunity to resume their married life. This does not mean that the tribunal will try to persuade a couple to reconcile, but it does place an onus on tribunal staff to ensure that there is no hope of reconciliation before they begin investigating the marriage for invalidity. Most tribunals will assume that any chance of reconciliation has passed if a secular divorce decree has been issued. This is one reason that most tribunals, without coercing them to do so, require that the couple have obtained a divorce before proceeding with an application for nullity.

Each tribunal has its own preferred method of responding to an application. Some will require the completion of forms to obtain necessary details and perhaps a short narrative about the marriage before the person is asked to attend an interview. Others will ask the petitioner to attend for a preliminary interview and later for a more in-depth interview. Some may proceed directly to a full interview. In some dioceses, arrangements can often be made for the applicant to be interviewed by his or her parish priest or by some other suitably trained person in the locality. Any potential applicant should contact the local tribunal for more information about its particular procedures.

Since the majority of applicants would require guidance in drawing up a formal petition, most tribunals undertake this task for them using information from the first interview or other details provided by the applicant. Once the petition has been read and amended as necessary, the applicant will be asked to sign the petition.

A typical petition might read as follows:

>18 Main Street,
>Any Town,
>Somewhere.

My Lord Bishop or Dear Bishop [name]

I, [name of petitioner], married [name of spouse] on 18 September 1999 at the church of All Saints, Any Town. I was 22 years old at the time and he was 23. We are both Catholics. We separated in January 2002 and were divorced on 4 June 2003.

We met at work when I was 19 and decided to live together. We were in love and I got pregnant. This wasn't intended. Our child was born on Christmas Day 1997. I wanted us to be a proper family and so pushed him for marriage. I don't think he wanted marriage but he agreed.

Even before we married, he was always out with his

friends. He was no help with our child and we were effectively living separate lives. Nothing changed when we married. He still went out and we were arguing more and more. Then I found out he had been seeing someone else and I asked him to leave.

In 2010, I met a man who has never been married before. We have lived together since 2012 and we want to marry. My faith is important to me.

Therefore, I petition the tribunal, competent by reason of the place of marriage, to declare my marriage to [name of spouse] null on the grounds that both of us were gravely lacking in discretionary judgement for marriage.

[Signed and dated by the petitioner]

The petition is usually addressed to the bishop in recognition of his status as head of the tribunal, although in practice he will rarely see it. It gives a brief outline of the marriage, the names of the parties, the place of marriage and relevant dates.

Ideally, the petition should also name the grounds to be examined. Most applicants would not know enough of canon law to suggest the possible grounds to be investigated in a particular case. Hence, it is likely that the tribunal will assist the applicant in writing the petition. The tribunal can suggest those grounds that seem likely to have a chance of being proved based on the limited information already presented. These grounds can be changed if later information indicates that others should be considered.

The presentation of the petition is the first phase of the process and forms the basis of the first decision to be made by the tribunal. At this point, the tribunal will make a judgement about the viability of the application and can reject a petition if the case appears to have no chance of reaching a successful conclusion. It is relatively rare for a petition to be rejected and, when it is, the reasons for rejection should be explained and details of how to appeal against that decision should be given. If an appeal against rejection is lodged, the appeal tribunal will examine the decision and may instruct the first tribunal to hear the case.

Since 2015, when Pope Francis changed the rules, besides the decision about accepting or rejecting the petition, the Judicial Vicar must also decide if the circumstances of the marriage might warrant the use of the new briefer process, which is explained in a later chapter. What is described here refers to the process used for most cases.

The most important evidence obtained in any application for nullity is usually that of the applicant. It is obtained during an interview in which the applicant, in response to a series of questions, is asked to speak about the relationship of the couple and the reasons for the breakdown of that relationship. A written record of the given responses will be made. Applicants should be asked to confirm that the written record accurately reflects what they have said.

Marriage is a relationship of two people, each of whom will have been formed by the experiences of his or her life before meeting the other. Consequently, the interviewer will ask for details of the backgrounds of the parties, their experiences of early family life and other relationships, any particular matters that might have affected their development, the courtship of the couple, their motives for marriage and their personalities, as well as requesting a history of the marriage and the reasons it ended in separation.

Unfortunately, it is sometimes necessary for these questions to be intrusive but, if essential, the tribunal can retain very sensitive information in complete confidence.

The results of this interview will form the major part of the petitioner's evidence. Sometimes it is supplemented by a statement submitted at the time of application or by information sent after the interview. Most of the evidence is collected in this way and it is only written evidence that is presented to the judges at the time they meet to decide the matter.

A matter of concern for many applying for nullity is the issue of confidentiality. Tribunals are bound to keep all their files in a secure location accessible only to tribunal personnel. The only people who might have access to what is said by the parties are tribunal personnel and those parties. Even then, it is possible that certain information may be considered so sensitive that it will not be shown to the other party. This might occur, for example, if one spouse had been unfaithful with a member of the other's family, or if one of them speaks of having been sexually abused but had never told the other of this during their marriage. The nullity process should not be used to reveal to the other party information that he or she had not otherwise come to know.

The tribunal is concerned with truth. Only if it is reasonably certain that the true and relevant facts have been revealed can it make a judgement about the validity of a particular marriage. It is for this reason that applicants are encouraged to speak freely about themselves, the marriage and its problems. It is also for this reason that others besides the petitioner are asked to give evidence.

It is appropriate to give some words of advice to anyone

who is thinking of making an application for nullity of marriage, or perhaps is already in the process of doing so. Following this advice will also assist the tribunal in handling your application.

DO

- Say if you would prefer not to be interviewed by any particular person. Some, for example, would prefer not to speak about personal matters with their parish priest, or a woman might prefer to be interviewed by another woman. The tribunal will try to accommodate such requests.
- Ask the tribunal staff if you want any explanation or information about the procedure.
- Discuss any concerns you may have about the process with the tribunal.
- Request a progress report if the tribunal has not contacted you for a while. However, remember that the procedure takes time to complete. Please be patient if you have been advised to wait.
- Answer promptly letters or other communications from the tribunal.
- Tell the whole truth. There is almost certainly nothing you can say that will not have been heard before by the tribunal staff.
- Assist the tribunal, and hence others who may wish to apply, by paying whatever you can towards the costs incurred.
- Inform the tribunal if, for any reason, you decide not to proceed with your application. The papers already collected will normally be filed away in case you should change your mind at a later date.
- Make a serious attempt to provide contact details for your former spouse. The next chapter will explain

why this is important.

DON'T
- Tell others what to say when they give evidence. Such could seriously jeopardise your chances of a successful outcome.
- Be afraid to approach the tribunal about taking up again a case that has lapsed.
- Expect tribunal staff or anyone else to tell you your application will succeed. There can be no certainty until a declaration of nullity is handed down and, no matter how promising your application may appear, tribunal staff will not be able to promise anything.

Chapter 16

The Respondent

In any nullity application, the 'respondent' is the title given to the other party to the marriage. This title simply means that the other party responds to the petition that requests the investigation into the validity of the marriage. It does not imply that the petitioner has made allegations about the respondent. It is useful to recall that grounds can be found in either the petitioner or the respondent or both. The eventual judgement concerns the validity of the marriage and is not intended as a judgement on the people concerned but on the situation that existed at the time of the wedding.

Unless there are children to whom both parties have access, it is unlikely that the couple will have remained in contact. Often, particularly if the divorce was acrimonious, even the thought of involving the other party in the nullity process might be quite repugnant to an applicant.

However, every marriage is between two people and both have a right to know that the validity of the marriage is being questioned. A successful application changes the canonical legal status of the marriage and so affects the canonical legal status of both parties.

Although the respondent has the right to be informed of the application and a right to take part in the process, the parties do not need to meet or to communicate with one another in any way. Nor will the tribunal communicate current personal information about one party to the other.

When presenting an application for nullity, the petitioner is expected to provide contact details for the respondent. This will hopefully include a postal address, although sometimes an email address will suffice if that is all that is available. If a personal address cannot be found, the address of a family member may suffice, on the assumption that any communication can be forwarded. It is only in extreme circumstances and after the tribunal is satisfied that the petitioner has made all reasonable efforts that an application can proceed without the respondent having been contacted directly.

Once a case is accepted for hearing, the potential grounds decided and a petition has been signed, the tribunal will contact the respondent and provide a copy of the petition. The respondent will be told that the application has been made and will be invited to participate in the process. Information as to how that can be done will be provided.

Respondents do not have to participate in the process and many will refuse to do so. Some choose to completely ignore the tribunal's communications. Others take some interest and a few will involve themselves to a considerable extent and may agree to be interviewed about the marriage using a questionnaire similar to that used for a petitioner.

Since the tribunal is seeking the objective truth of the matter, receiving some evidence from the respondent can be useful. This might be done by means of an interview in person but might also be done over the internet or by telephone. Sometimes, questions can be sent by post or by email and answers returned the same way. Such can assist the possibility of obtaining some information, although these latter means of providing it can restrict the value of the evidence obtained.

Informing a respondent that a former spouse is applying for nullity sometimes provokes adverse reactions. Some respondents claim they do not believe that marriages can be declared invalid. Others claim that participating in the process seems too much like raking up the past. To some, it feels like a personal attack. To others, it seems too much of a personal matter to be subjected to the scrutiny of outsiders. Some perceive the process as irrelevant and unnecessary and wonder why their former spouses cannot simply remarry without involving them. Others will state a strong belief that the marriage was valid and will refuse to assist with a process that might decide otherwise.

A respondent might object to the fact of an application, but he or she cannot prevent the investigation from occurring. After all, the truth of the validity or otherwise of the marriage is an historical fact and the purpose of the investigation is to try to discover that truth. That truth does not depend on the wishes or feelings of either party.

Once it has commenced, only the petitioner can withdraw the petition and so call a halt to the proceedings. Sometimes it happens that a petitioner does ask for the process to be stopped only for the respondent to wish it to continue. In those circumstances, the respondent effectively becomes the petitioner.

Tribunals will often suggest that the petitioner, if able to do so, should notify the respondent of the application for a declaration of nullity of the marriage. The tribunal's letter informing the respondent of the application will not then come as a surprise and the respondent may be more willing to assist. Of course, not all applicants would want to have such contact with the former spouse.

The right to have the status of the marriage examined, subject to acceptance of the case by the tribunal, belongs to both parties. It is a right to an investigation, not a right to a declaration of nullity. The petitioner is simply the party who first makes the request. Neither party receives preferential treatment. The respondent, like the petitioner, has the right to name witnesses and have legal representation.

If a respondent objects to the proceedings, the tribunal will note the objection but will still proceed if it believes there are grounds to do so; namely, that there appears to be a chance that the marriage may be null. Justice might be thwarted if one party had the right to call a halt to the proceedings without the consent of the other.

When a respondent was the cause of breakdown of the marriage, it can happen that assisting the former spouse with his or her application for nullity is seen as an opportunity for contrition. Some respondents can be honest enough to recognise the part they played in bringing unhappiness into the life of the petitioner or the breakdown of the marriage. Confessing their failings to the tribunal can make a valuable contribution to healing old wounds.

Similarly, when a respondent feels that he or she was the wronged party, assisting the tribunal might be seen as an opportunity to have the truth recognised by an independent third party.

Both parties have rights in the nullity process and these are:
- The right to petition to have the marriage investigated, although not to have the petition accepted.
- The right to appeal against a rejection of petition.
- The right to be notified that the marriage is being investigated for invalidity.
- The right to be informed of the grounds for nullity that are being examined in the case.
- The right to present evidence.
- The right to name witnesses and to know the names of the witnesses put forward by the other.
- The right to be informed of the names of the judges who will hear the case.
- The right to assistance in the process from an advocate or procurator (advocates, however, are not always available and a party requesting the use of an advocate might be required to pay a fee for those services).
- The right, at the appropriate stage of the process, to read and comment on the evidence supplied by the other party and any witnesses. The instructing judge, however, has a right to withhold some evidence when there is good reason to do so.
- The right to be notified of the tribunal's decision.
- The right to have a copy of the tribunal's judgement (the sentence) made available. This will aid an

understanding of the reasons for the judgement and may assist in making a decision about whether or not to appeal.
- The right to appeal against the judgement, either to the immediate appeal tribunal or directly to the Roman Rota. The appeal tribunal can, however, reject a request for an appeal hearing if such a request is not appropriately justified.

These rights are important and, if not respected, can in some circumstances lead to the tribunal's judgement being declared null.

When a respondent feels aggrieved about an application, discussing the matter with a member of the tribunal staff might alleviate some concerns. Respondents, too, can be offered advice:

DO
- Ask for assistance in understanding the process and its implications.
- Have the courtesy to answer the tribunal's citation, even if only to register your lack of interest in the matter.
- Recognise that your status before the tribunal is no less than that of your former spouse.

DON'T
- Take out your anger on tribunal staff. They are only doing their duty and will assist you as readily as they will assist your former spouse.
- Presume that your lack of cooperation will obstruct the process and prevent a decree of nullity being issued.
- Assume that the investigation is a personal attack

because your former spouse made the application. Remember the grounds can be in either party.
- Presume, if you are not a Catholic, that the process is irrelevant to you. Should it happen that you should wish to marry a practicing Catholic in future, the outcome of the nullity proceedings would have important implications for you.

Chapter 17

Providing Proof of Nullity

Anyone who puts a matter of contention before a court is expected to provide the proof of his or her cause. Hence, it is the responsibility of the person who applies for nullity to prove that the marriage is null.

That may appear a daunting task but it is not as difficult as it might appear. For one thing, the tribunal's role is to deliver a just decision and that means there is an onus on tribunal personnel, as an important part of their ministry, to assist the petitioner to present the truth by asking appropriate questions and offering helpful guidance.

When Pope Francis made adjustments to the law in 2015 in relation to the marriage nullity process, he enshrined in the written law an important aspect of natural law. Recognising that the majority of people who apply for nullity do so for spiritual reasons – they want to live in peace with God in the decisions they make in life – the law now states in essence that, unless there is reason to think otherwise, petitioners are to be believed when they are speaking about the circumstances of their previous marriages.

Nevertheless, tribunals cannot find in favour of nullity unless the judges are sure that the truth of the marriage has been revealed. Evidence from the respondent might help them to reach that certainty, but it is also possible that the two parties might give conflicting evidence and this can lead to some confusion about where the truth lies.

Tribunals usually require the petitioner to name some witnesses. The evidence they give can assist the tribunal in being certain that the truth is revealed.

Both parties can name witnesses and the petitioner is usually expected to name a few. The number of witnesses is not as important as the quality of the evidence each can give about the marriage and the parties. One good witness can be of greater value to a case than a number who offer little by way of evidence. Some tribunals ask the parties to name just two or three witnesses, whilst others will ask for more. The evidence of two or three good witnesses is usually quite sufficient.

Witnesses can be anyone, of any religion or none, who have knowledge of the parties and their marriage. In the majority of applications, the most obvious witnesses will be family members; parents, siblings, grandparents and even on occasion a child from the marriage. Close friends or others in whom the parties have confided can also be very useful. Since it is the time of the wedding that is ultimately important – it was at that moment that the marriage either did or did not come into existence – it is preferable that witnesses knew the couple at that time.

Before naming witnesses, the parties should ensure that the people they nominate are willing to act in that capacity. Most family members and friends are only too happy to help. As with the petitioner, the evidence of witnesses is gathered by means of an interview. Again, different tribunals adopt different procedures. Some advise that witnesses should come to the tribunal office for interview, while others arrange for witnesses to be interviewed in their own homes or another convenient place. It happens on occasion that witnesses are interviewed over the telephone, via the internet, or even by sending questions through the post or by email. These latter means of collecting evidence are not ideal, as it is impossible to be certain that the collected evidence is solely the work of the person concerned.

A written transcript of the witness's evidence has to be prepared for submission to the judges. Hence, the interview with the witness will be recorded in some way and the witness will be asked to sign a document as proof that the given evidence is authentic. Witnesses are often asked to give their evidence under oath.

Witnesses can be apprehensive about what is required. Some witnesses are concerned that they do not know enough about the marriage and others that they might let the petitioner down or might break confidences. Of course, witnesses can only state what they know about the parties and the marriage. Some may have had a close relationship with one or both of the parties, while others will have been only casual observers. In order to ensure that witnesses reveal as much as they know, a questionnaire will be used for the interview. The questions may be wide-ranging, covering such areas as the personalities and backgrounds of the parties, events before the marriage, events during the marriage and the reasons for the breakdown.

Witnesses are encouraged to give full evidence. They are requested to state opinions and hearsay evidence, as well as facts they have learned for themselves. The judges will determine what weight is to be attached to particular aspects of the evidence collected. Many tribunals have volunteer lay people who have been trained in the role of auditor. It is the auditor's role to record the witness's testimony and present it to the tribunal.

Sometimes, documentary evidence can be supplied. For example, a woman who claims that she was consistently beaten and needed medical attention might be able to obtain confirmation of that fact from her doctor.

Sometimes, tribunals will ask for a psychiatric or psychological evaluation of one or both parties by an appropriately trained professional. The resultant report can be useful in evaluating how well the person may have functioned in a marital relationship.

It can happen that petitioners are not able to provide witnesses or that the evidence available from the witnesses does not provide sufficient corroboration of the petitioner's story. This can happen for many reasons; for example, the petitioner might be a very private person or may have moved around so much that nobody had close contact with the couple for long. When witnesses are not available, it might be possible to obtain character references; that is, people who have no knowledge of the marriage, but who can attest to the truthfulness and integrity of one or both parties.

When all the evidence is collected, the parties will be given an opportunity to read and comment on the evidence. This stage of the process is known as 'publication of the acts', although actual publication extends only to the parties, their advocates and those tribunal personnel working on the case. Publication has to occur at the offices of a tribunal to avoid danger of confidentiality being jeopardised, although exceptions to this general principle are occasionally allowed. This stage of the process allows the parties to discover what the other and the witnesses have said about them. It allows them to answer allegations, correct any misleading information or give a correct interpretation where a false impression currently exists. If this right to view the acts is to be exercised and to preserve the integrity of the process, most tribunals insist that an oath of confidentiality is signed before the evidence is shown to the parties for their comment.

At this time, it is appropriate that an assessment of the case should be made by an experienced canon lawyer whose function will be to make a judgement about the sufficiency of the evidence; sufficiency meaning adequate to allow appropriate certainty that the relevant facts have been revealed. This assessment will normally be made by the instructing judge. Where the evidence is deemed insufficient, it is appropriate that attempts are made to obtain additional information and this is best done before publication occurs.

It is possible in some rare circumstances for some evidence to be given in total confidence. This might occur if harm could arise from the evidence becoming known; for example, a petitioner's mother might have loaned money to the respondent that was never repaid and does not want her daughter to find out in case she feels obliged to repay that money. When evidence is given in confidence, there is always an underlying suspicion that it may be false. The judges will have to make an assessment of whether or not that confidential information is reliable. Knowing the reason for the request that it is withheld can be useful in making that assessment. It is possible for revelations by one party to be withheld from the other if, for example, scandal or grave damage might occur if they were made known.

After the publication, a decree of conclusion is signed by the instructing judge. This effectively means no more evidence can be admitted and the tribunal personnel then begin to prepare their legal arguments in preparation for judgement.

Chapter 18

Concluding the Process

The formal process for examining marriages for possible invalidity can be divided roughly into four stages: the presentation and acceptance of the petition, the collection of the evidence, the presentation of arguments for and against nullity and the judgement. This chapter explains the third and fourth stages of the process and examines the roles played by various tribunal personnel.

The roles that are discussed here are those of advocate, procurator, defender of the bond and judge. All will have some expertise in the law of the Church relating to marriage nullity. Historically, these roles have all largely been fulfilled by priests, being the only people appropriately trained in canon law. It is perhaps only in the last 50 years that Religious Sisters and, later still, other lay people have obtained appropriate canonical expertise to assist in this work. However, there does not appear to be any theological reason that would prevent lay people being appointed to any position or office in ecclesiastical tribunals, even though canon law does not currently allow this. Pope Francis made an important change in 2015 by allowing two of the three judges in any particular case to be lay people, thereby recognising that ordination is not a pre-requisite to giving effect to decisions in relation to marriage nullity.

Advocates can be used in marriage nullity cases to assist either party to present the best case for nullity or, if acting for a respondent, potentially for arguing against nullity. In many tribunals, the use of advocates is rarely considered necessary; the facts speak for themselves. However, some tribunals use advocates routinely. They might assist, for example, when nullity is not obviously proved, perhaps at an appeal stage. They might also be useful in providing advice and counsel to a respondent who feels particularly aggrieved at the possibility of a declaration of nullity. When all the evidence in a marriage nullity case has been collected, advocates for the petitioner and respondent, if they are appointed, will present legal arguments in support of the cause of their respective clients.

A procurator will be appointed to act on behalf of one of the parties when that person is impeded from exercising his or her rights in the nullity process. This might occur if the party is seriously ill or perhaps is imprisoned.

When each advocate has presented written arguments, the defender of the bond will examine the case and present observations, again in writing. A defender of the bond must act at every grade of trial in marriage nullity cases.

As the title suggests, the defender of the bond effectively

acts for the Church in ensuring, as far as possible, that the teaching of Jesus on the permanence of marriage is upheld. It is the defender's role to explain to the judges why they might find nullity of the marriage not proved. Obviously, if a bond of marriage exists, it should be defended in these matters.

In Church publications, both the defender of the bond and the judges are described as 'ministers of justice'; a title that recognises their duty to strive for justice, which includes ensuring that justice is not thwarted. Hence, it is not the defender's role to persuade the judges to give a decision against nullity. The defender has to protect truth. The defender will present to the judges those genuine reasons that might justify them finding nullity not proved. However, a defender commenting on a marriage that is obviously null can simply remit the case to the justice of the court.

The defender also has a role much earlier in the process, including the right to be present at any interview to ensure that it is being conducted fairly. The defender may also direct that additional questions should be asked of the parties or their witnesses in order to clarify the evidence. This same right belongs to advocates.

The observations presented by both the defender and the advocate act as guidance for the judges, who will weigh them carefully but may dismiss them as lacking in solid foundation or even irrelevant.

In most tribunals, three judges will meet to decide if nullity is proved in a particular case. In some tribunals, however, when the bishop might struggle to appoint sufficient judges, he can allow the decisions to be made by just one judge, sometimes with the assistance or guidance of another canon lawyer.

When there are three judges, the majority verdict prevails. It is then the task of one of them to write the sentence; that is, to explain in a written document the rationale behind the decision they have reached. A sentence is usually in three parts: a summary of the facts relating to the marriage, its breakdown and the application for nullity; a brief resumé of the law pertinent to the grounds being examined; and, an explanation of why the judges believe the decision they have reached is appropriate to the given facts.

In their deliberations, the judges make decisions about two areas of doubt. Before they can decide about the validity of the marriage, they have to be morally certain that the truth of the matter is before them. Without that certainty, it is impossible for them to judge if invalidity is proved.

The judges sit alone and form their opinions only from the written evidence and written legal observations placed before them. The law does not allow anyone else to be present to argue either for or against the nullity of the marriage. The next chapter examines the judges' decision in more detail.

Chapter 19

Judgement and Appeal

Canon law presumes that every marriage is valid, even when neither party is a baptised Catholic. Even if a marriage appears obviously invalid, that invalidity is not formally recognised until such time as a decree of nullity is issued or the parties are otherwise declared free to remarry. That will only occur after the situation has been properly investigated by appropriate officials of the Church using one of the approved processes.

In each situation in which the validity of a marriage is questioned, the judges' task is to decide if the presented evidence is sufficient to establish invalidity. Thus, typical questions that the judges might consider are:
- Is it proved that this marriage is invalid on the ground that the petitioner was gravely lacking in discretion of judgement regarding the essential matrimonial rights

and obligations to be mutually given and accepted?
- Is it proved that this marriage is invalid on the ground that the respondent had an intention against children?
- Is it proved that this marriage is invalid because of lack of form?

The answer given by the judges is either affirmative or negative; that is, either invalidity is proved or it is not proved. When the answer is negative, it is not appropriate to interpret this as meaning that the marriage is valid. Of course, the marriage may be valid but the judgement is a statement only that invalidity was not proved.

When nullity is found not proved, the presumption of law that the marriage is valid remains in force. In other words, nothing has changed as a result of the judgement. The legal status of the marriage remains 'presumed valid'. However, the possibility is not denied that the presumption is wrong. No court can deliver a perfect judgement every time and tribunals of the Catholic Church are no exception. The court can base its decisions only on the evidence put before it. If that evidence does not reveal truth, there is a risk that the court's judgement will be wrong.

When the judges decide that a marriage is invalid, this is not necessarily the end of the matter. Once the tribunal's judgement is notified to the parties, a right of appeal commences. An appeal can be made only by one of the parties to the marriage or by the defender of the bond. The appeal is lodged with the tribunal that made the judgement against which the appeal is made.

An appeal has to be presented within a strict period of time. The law states within 15 working days and this time period begins when the parties are notified of the judgement and the sentence becomes available for inspection. An opportunity must be given for the tribunal's decision to be examined, which effectively means making the sentence available for scrutiny. In some tribunals, the judgement is made but it might take the judge some weeks to write the sentence and make it available. The time period for appeal cannot commence until the sentence is made available, for the obvious reason that, without the sentence, it can be difficult to know if a decision to appeal is appropriate. Furthermore, the sentence may assist the appellant in knowing how to formulate the appeal. However, an appeal can be lodged whether or not the sentence is read. If no appeal against an affirmative decision is lodged within the time allowed, the right of appeal is lost and a decree of nullity of the marriage is issued.

After a judgement that nullity is not proved, a right of appeal also commences. These marriage nullity cases are matters that concern the 'status of persons' and what is also implicitly being questioned when a marriage is examined for nullity is the marital status of the spouses. Questions concerning the status of persons are never formally settled, since the truth of such matters is of great importance. However, there are rules that prevent the same person repeatedly presenting the same question to Church courts. The point is this: even if a tribunal does not find nullity proved in a particular case, it is usually possible to have that decision reviewed at least once and at any time in the future.

Pope Francis introduced another innovation in 2015 and this means that, if an appeal is lodged, the first decision of an appeal tribunal concerns acceptance of the appeal. The appeal tribunal can reject an appeal if it believes that it has been lodged merely to delay the issuance of a decree of nullity. Hence, when presenting an appeal, it is important to explain carefully why a second hearing is requested.

When an appeal is accepted, there will be a second full formal hearing of the case. However, an appeal tribunal does not start the process from the beginning. The evidence and legal arguments already collected will be used again. The appeal tribunal might introduce new grounds to be heard alongside any grounds that have already been judged and the parties will be asked if they want to provide additional evidence, either themselves or through witnesses.

One judge in the appeal tribunal will be assigned the role of instructing the case and he or she will make a careful assessment of the evidence already collected and form an opinion as to the justice of the first decision. This judge may direct that one or both parties should be asked specific questions about a particular aspect of their marital relationship or that specific evidence should be gathered. This can result in important information becoming known at the appeal stage that was not known to the judges of first instance.

Sometimes, it can be recognised that the evidence produced from an interview for the first hearing did not provide enough of a full and balanced picture of the marriage. It has been known for a more useful picture to be presented when a petitioner has been asked to write, in his or her own time at home, a statement about the courtship and marriage and the couple's relationship. This can provide important nuances that might be missed in the context of a formal interview. Such a statement, signed and attested as truthful, can be an important element of proof. When suggesting that such a statement is written, the instructing judge can provide guidance to a petitioner by suggesting those matters or areas of the relationship about which the person should write. The complexity of human relationships means that subtle behavioural traits that might normally not affect more casual relationships can be significant when it comes to the intimate interpersonal relationship that is the foundation stone of true marriage. Giving proper expression to the damaging effects of some traits of personality is not always easy.

Once all the new evidence is gathered, the appeal tribunal proceeds in the same way as the first tribunal. The evidence is published, the tribunal officers and advocates present their briefs and the judgement is made and notified to the parties. In the event that the appeal tribunal agrees with the previous judgement on any particular ground for nullity, no further appeal is possible. Hence, whenever the judgement of both tribunals has found nullity proved on even one ground, the decree of nullity can be issued without delay. When a previous decision is reversed or a pronouncement is made on a new ground for nullity, then there would be a right of appeal against the decision and it would have to be exercised within the short period of time allowed by the law.

If another appeal is made, the case must be sent to a third tribunal. This will usually be the Rota in Rome. Should this eventuality arise, the local tribunal will be able to guide the petitioner with appropriate information.

Chapter 20

The Briefer Process

When, in 2015, Pope Francis made changes to the law that regulates the nullity process, he was responding in part to a request from the Synod of Bishops that the nullity process should be simplified so that decisions could be made more quickly. Of course, such aspirations have to be balanced against the need to discover truth, achieve justice and respect rights.

Amongst those changes was the possibility of using a briefer process when particular circumstances exist. In situations in which the briefer process can be used, it should be possible for a declaration of nullity to be issued within just two to three months.

The briefer process can be used only when certain conditions are fulfilled and such conditions will necessarily restrict the use of this process. One condition is that the initial presentation of the case to the tribunal should indicate that nullity of the marriage appears obvious. Examples of when nullity might appear obvious are: the marriage lasted a very short period of time; one of the parties seriously misled the other before marriage about important facts; or, one of the parties continued in an adulterous relationship even after taking marriage promises. It is the responsibility of the Judicial Vicar to decide if the circumstances outlined by a petitioner might indicate obvious nullity and so if the briefer process might be used.

Another condition for the use of the brief process is that both parties to the marriage agree in principle that the marriage should be declared invalid. The law envisages the possibility that a joint petition might be signed by a couple who were married. Much more likely in reality is that the Judicial Vicar will recognise, from a request by one party for a declaration of nullity, that the briefer process might be used and so he will seek the consent of the other party to proceed with the briefer process. In such cases, the Judicial Vicar is to send a copy of the petition to the respondent and invite the respondent to comment. If the respondent does not reply, the briefer process cannot be used. In order to use the briefer process, both parties must respond positively to the notion that the marriage might be declared invalid. Consent in these matters cannot be presumed.

Hence, for the briefer process to be used, the respondent has to agree that the marriage should be declared invalid. The respondent has to take an active part in the process, even if that assistance is limited only to providing written agreement with the contents of the petition.

It is important that each party agrees both with the alleged facts that could give rise to nullity and the proposed grounds upon which the validity of the marriage is to be challenged. It might happen, for example, that they agree their marriage lasted only two months but completely disagree about why it broke down so quickly. Each might blame the other and so, whilst it might be said that they agree that the marriage is null, they obviously do not agree on the cause of nullity. Hence, there is likely to be disagreement concerning the grounds upon which nullity might be declared. In such circumstances, the briefer process should not be used. A full formal process will be necessary to establish the truth.

Another important aspect of the briefer process is that the judge for the case will be the bishop of the diocese. He is the first judge in every diocese but would rarely act in that capacity in cases of marriage nullity. Nevertheless, the Holy Father did not want to give any impression that the briefer process was undermining the Church's teaching that marriage is for life and so he decided it was appropriate to have the full weight of local ecclesiastical authority behind these judgements. The case, however, is prepared by the Judicial Vicar or another judge and the bishop has to take advice from other canon lawyers, known as assessors, when making his decision.

In theory, the evidence in these cases should be collected quickly and need only be in summary form, focussing on the matter that appears to give rise to nullity. The defender of the bond will present any observations, as will any advocates who have been appointed. The bishop will then either decide nullity is certain and so give his judgement in a brief sentence or he can decide that nullity is not proved to his satisfaction and so he will determine that a full formal hearing is to occur. Hence, the bishop never gives a formal decision that nullity is not proved. A decision against nullity will only ever be made after a full formal hearing.

By reason of these being obvious cases for nullity and that both parties have consented to the marriage being declared null, an appeal is unlikely. Nevertheless, an appeal by one of the parties or the defender of the bond is possible and such an appeal has to be made within the allotted time. Once that time has expired and if no appeal has been lodged, a decree of nullity will be issued.

Chapter 21

Other Matters Pertinent to the Nullity Process

What changes?

A declaration of marriage nullity changes just one thing: the legal status of the parties to the marriage. When a decree of nullity is issued, the marriage ceases to have legal effect. That is the only public effect of a decree of nullity.

The decree of nullity does nothing but change the interpretation in law of the status of the parties. On the wedding day, their status in law changed from unmarried to married. In truth, however, their status did not change. The nullity decree recognises that there was no true marriage and so the spouses never actually married, even if they did have a union that the law and the public recognised as a marriage.

The tribunal's judgement, which is given legal effect by the decree of nullity, cannot change anything else. The facts that gave rise to the invalidity of the marriage are historical truth and that cannot change. The tribunal's judgement is simply a legal interpretation of those facts.

Of course, the perception of people regarding the marriage will also likely change when a decree of nullity is issued. A decree of nullity can bring relief, a sense of peace, or comfort in other ways to the people concerned. It can open up possibilities for the future.

Remarriage

Once the nullity decree is signed, both parties are usually free to remarry. Marriage breakdown and its causes can be very traumatic for the spouses and it can happen that a tribunal will suggest that one or both should undertake some counselling or other pastoral assistance before remarrying. In extreme cases, the tribunal can advise that remarriage should not occur. This might happen when a person manifested behaviour that had such a damaging effect on the spouse that any future marriage is likely to fail for the same reason as the first.

Time and Costs

If the tribunal system consistently fails in anything, it is in processing nullity cases quickly and efficiently. Canon law suggests that tribunals should process a case in first instance within one year. If an appeal is lodged, canon law states that the second hearing should be completed within a further six months. The briefer process should be completed within just a few months. Some tribunals can act within these limits but many seem unable to do so.

It is the responsibility of the bishop to ensure his tribunal is adequately equipped with appropriately trained personnel and other resources. The current requirements of the law are that some of these personnel are ordained. Given that those willing to be ordained are becoming fewer in many countries and they often have other demands on their time, bishops will find it more and more difficult to fill tribunal vacancies. Lay people qualified in canon law are few. Those who do obtain relevant qualifications may struggle to find appropriate employment and not every diocese would be able to pay salaries commensurate with the skills that such employees would bring to the task.

When he made changes to the process in 2015, the Holy Father advised that, where possible, nullity applications should be processed free of charge. Clearly, he wants the nullity process accessible to everyone. However, most tribunals have always provided a free service to those who cannot afford to pay.

Most dioceses attempt to fund their tribunals by asking petitioners for a contribution towards the cost of processing their applications. Operating tribunals is expensive and finance has to be found from somewhere. Asking those who can afford to do so to pay something towards the cost is not unreasonable. The cost of having the marriage declared invalid is very small in comparison to the cost of a wedding. It would seem safe to say that nobody should be deterred from making an application because of an inability to pay. Any potential applicant who is concerned about costs should contact the appropriate tribunal for information.

Status of Children

A matter of concern to some is the status of their children after a declaration of nullity. Their reasoning is as follows: nullity means we were never married and so, since our children were not born within a marriage, they must be illegitimate.

That is not the case. Legitimacy is a statement about the legal status of children. The term 'legitimate' means within the law. Hence, in this context, illegitimate means outside a lawful marriage. It does not mean outside a valid marriage. Every wedding produces a legal marriage but that marriage may or may not be valid. A marriage that is later declared invalid nevertheless remains lawful until the decree of nullity is issued and will be recognised as having been lawful for the period between the date of the wedding and the date of the decree of nullity. Hence, children born within that marriage are born within the law and so are legitimate. The subsequent declaration that the marriage was invalid does not change the legal status of the children.

Situations of Multiple Previous Marriages

When an application for nullity is made after there have been two or more previous marriages, the situation can become complicated. An applicant who is not a Catholic would need to apply for a declaration of nullity of each previous marriage. This can result in one person having two or more applications before the same tribunal at the same time and each would have to result in a declaration of nullity if the person was to be declared free to remarry.

If, however, the person with more than one previous marriage was a baptised Catholic at the time of the first marriage, the problem of multiple prior marriages should not arise. Any Catholic attempting second marriage without a declaration that the first was invalid would have to do so outside the Church and so the subsequent marriage could be declared to have been invalid because of lack of form.

There is no limit to the number of declarations of nullity of marriage that a person might obtain. Nevertheless, the nature of marriage requires a personal self-gift for the whole of life. Those who appropriately make that gift and then suffer marital breakdown will require time to heal and psychological scars are likely to remain. These can have an impact upon any future marriage. The possibility of making that necessary gift, after a person has suffered multiple marriage failures, might be questioned. Yet, the potential for healing arising from a subsequent true marriage can be significant and might be recognised as a gift from God.

An overview

The tribunal system and marriage nullity process sometimes receive a bad press. The procedure can be perceived as excessively secretive, extremely slow, a waste of human and other resources, and unpleasantly intrusive. Unfortunately, these criticisms are not always without foundation. Tribunal personnel will attempt to handle cases with empathy and understanding, but they are not infallible.

The tribunal judges would be neglecting their duty and the trust placed in them by their bishop if they did not apply the law equitably and justly. In their approach to the parties, they will be pastoral and sensitive. However, when it comes to making a judicial decision, they are seeking truth. That means that some applications for nullity will not fulfil the requirements of the law for a decree of nullity to be granted.

There is no doubt that some people have had legitimate cause to complain about the way tribunals have handled their applications. However, there is also no doubt that many more have benefited greatly from being able to talk openly and honestly about their failed marriages, realising that they are not unique in the pain they endured in marriage and its breakdown and being freed to search for God's will in a new relationship, if the application is successful. The process is not without some discomfort or even pain, although much of this might be attributed to lingering effects of the breakdown of the marriage rather than to the nullity process itself. Hence, whilst a nullity application can revive buried hurts, the potential for healing is significant.

The nullity process will never solve all the problems that can arise from a broken marriage. Whilst some petitioners state that they received great personal benefit from their experience of having the marriage examined for possible nullity, the process is primarily designed to discover and safeguard justice and truth, whilst respecting rights. Interviews with the parties may present an opportunity for some limited counselling but the primary purpose of the nullity process is to reveal truth and allow justice, not to heal the scars of a broken marriage or to ensure that the parties are prepared for a future marriage.

Whilst it is hoped that all who have suffered marriage breakdown will seek assistance in preparing themselves appropriately before attempting another marriage, those whose applications fail are especially advised to seek spiritual guidance and counselling to assist them in an understanding of their situation within the Church.

SECTION III

Chapter 22

Marriage Dissolution in the Church

Non-consummation and Petrine Privilege Cases

Sometimes, even though the other spouse is still alive, it is possible to remarry without having a previous marriage declared invalid. If a marriage was never consummated or if one of the parties to the marriage was not baptised, the Pope will sometimes use the power that is unique to his office to dissolve the bond of marriage and thus allow a second marriage to be celebrated.

Because these particular cases do not involve a declaration of nullity, it can be said that they are as close to divorce as is possible in the Catholic Church. Christ taught that divorce is not possible. Yet, He also gave to Peter, the apostle, and his successors, the Popes, the power 'to bind and to loose'. Hence these cases are generally known as Petrine Privilege cases.

Non-consummation of a marriage can occur for many reasons. Consummation is considered essential to the fulness of a marriage. Unless the two spouses become physically one body in the sexual act, they are not married in the full sense of the word. When a non-consummated marriage breaks down, one or both of the parties can request the Church to dissolve the bond of that marriage by using the special procedures laid down for such cases.

Although it is the Holy Father who grants the dissolution, it is the local bishop or his delegate who is responsible for processing the application and preparing the papers to be sent to Rome. The procedures are such that the non-consummation must be proved beyond reasonable doubt. These matters are by their nature intrusive and so applicants whose marriages were not consummated usually prefer to petition for a decree of nullity, rather than for dissolution.

A sacramental marriage occurs when both spouses are baptised. When one of the parties to a marriage is not baptised, the marriage is not a sacrament according to the theology of the Church. A sacrament is, after all, a sign; a sign of interior grace. When a person is not baptised, it is assumed that he or she is not a Christian and so would not signal Christian beliefs. Marriages in which only one person or neither is baptised are recognised as true in every sense of the word; just not sacramental. In some circumstances, the Pope will grant the favour of dissolving the bond of a non-sacramental marriage when that marriage has ended prematurely.

One of the conditions for the use of this favour is that the granting of the privilege will assist the faith of a Catholic. So, for example, it might be used when an unbaptised person's marriage has failed and the person now wishes to marry a Catholic who was not previously married and whose faith is important. The case is prepared locally and the papers are forwarded to Rome with a recommendation from the local bishop. The local diocese will advise applicants if this process might be used in their particular circumstances.

The important distinction to bear in mind is that these are dissolutions and not declarations of nullity. The Church presumes that a valid bond of marriage exists and the Holy Father can use his office to dissolve that bond. He does this as a favour to assist the faith of a Catholic and is more likely to look favourably on such a request if the marriage being dissolved gives some appearance of also having been invalid.

Pauline Privilege Cases

There is another situation in which the dissolution of the bond of a non-sacramental marriage is possible; namely, when the marriage is between two people who are not baptised and one subsequently receives baptism. It is another situation that is allowed because it will assist the faith of a believer. The principle is found in St. Paul's first letter to the Corinthians (7:12-16) and is known as the Pauline Privilege. The privilege allows one of the parties to receive baptism and enter a second marriage providing he or she does not continue with the first marriage after the baptism and providing the other party does not wish to continue with the marriage. This process does not require the intervention of the Pope. Again, the local diocese will advise applicants if this process might be used in their particular circumstances.

Chapter 23

The Internal Forum Solution

This final chapter examines the situation of second marriage when a formal solution, such as a declaration of nullity, appears unlikely or impossible. Some people are not able to apply for a declaration of nullity of a previous marriage. The tribunal system is not accessible to everyone; for example, a person who would find it too difficult to speak of personal matters to a stranger. Others do apply but for one reason or another do not succeed in obtaining such a declaration.

All people are called in some way to be ministers in accordance with their specific vocation; that is, to provide a ministry to others in fulfilment of the basic Gospel commandments to love God and one's neighbour. The ministers in marriage, for example, are the spouses themselves. Other examples of ministry are: caring for the elderly, sick or imprisoned, parenting, teaching and, indeed, providing any service that helps others with their everyday needs.

Some of the baptised, such as priests or deacons, have a direct ministry of helping others in their spiritual lives; that is, to give direct assistance to others in their relationship with God. These ministers, appointed by the institution of the Church, will sometimes find themselves with the apparent dilemma of trying to reconcile pastoral practice with official Church teaching. How are they to respond to a woman who says she regularly uses contraception and feels that God understands? What are they to say to a man who is asking to receive the sacraments, when he is in his second marriage? Is it appropriate to deny the Eucharist to a couple who are known to be living together without marriage? In situations such as these, the people concerned must be presumed to be acting in good conscience. The ministers always have to respect the autonomy of those to whom they provide ministry because, ultimately, it is the individual believer who is responsible for fostering his or her relationship with God.

Matters of individual conscience are sometimes referred to as matters of the internal forum. Canon law and Church teaching in general apply first of all to the external forum; that is, what is known in the public domain. Yet, they also seek to educate and inform the internal forum and, as such, assist individuals in their decisions before God by developing their awareness of the relationship between God and His people.

Many Catholics are choosing to remarry after a failed marriage without first applying for a declaration of nullity or other solution. Of course, the second wedding cannot take place in the Church because the person is still considered bound to the promises made on the first wedding day. The Church cannot recognise the second marriage as a marriage because to do so would give an appearance of condoning an action contrary to the teaching of Jesus. So, these second marriages are often referred to as 'irregular unions', rather than marriages.

These situations can result in a lack of reconciliation of the internal and external fora. In the external forum, once a marriage has been celebrated, the spouses are prohibited from exchanging consent to marriage to another person because each is already married. In the internal forum, the first marriage is perceived as having ended and the person has exchanged consent to marriage with another because that seemed the right course of action to take; in other words, the person does not feel he or she is doing anything wrong or has acted in good conscience. Indeed, the remarried person may feel a much greater sense of peace and interior fulfilment within the second marriage than was ever the case with the first and such things can be a sign that the person is at one with God; that is, conforming his/her life to God's will. Such could also be an indication that there was something seriously wrong with the first marriage.

Nobody has a right to judge that a person living in an irregular union is in a state of sin. Christ taught that a person who remarries after divorce has committed adultery and so official Church teaching does state that such situations are sinful. Nevertheless, whereas that is the general teaching of the Church, no person has a right to stand in judgement over any specific second marriage, except the people who are party to that marriage.

That has to be right because, if the person is living in good conscience with the decision to remarry, it is possible that the person is actually following the will of God. After all, one way in which God speaks to us is through our consciences (cf. Vatican II, *Gaudium et Spes*, n.16). Anyone who intervenes in such matters risks standing in judgement of God.

It is important to appreciate that there can be a difference between the truth of a person's status and the canonical interpretation of that person's status. Hence, if a person who is in a second marriage should successfully apply for a declaration that the first marriage was null, the reality that the person is in truth married to the second spouse can be recognised by the Church. Therefore, if in truth the person is married to the second spouse, how can the second marriage be a sinful situation?

Before that declaration of nullity, the legal interpretation of the situation was that the person was already married and so was impeded from entering a second marriage. What that declaration of nullity does, in effect, is allow recognition that the legal interpretation of the situation did not accord with the truth of the situation. The reality was that the person, although legally impeded, was not in truth impeded from entering the second union. That reality existed by virtue of the first marriage being null, whether or not the Church declared it as such. The truth of that situation depends on the first marriage being null; not on that nullity actually being declared. If the first marriage was null, it was not a marriage and the second union is, in reality, the first and only marriage.

To put this another way, canonical status is not always a reliable guide to God's truth. The canonical status of people who are party to a wedding is determined by the legal presumption that all marriages are valid, even though we know that some are not. Hence, in some of these irregular union situations, when the first marriage was invalid, it is the Church's interpretation of the union that needs to change, not the person's situation in life.

Acknowledgement of this potential anomaly between the general teaching of the Church and a particular person's situation in life gives rise to something called the 'internal forum solution'. One benefit of applying this solution is that Church ministers can avoid having to judge those in second or irregular unions, as they can rely on the autonomy of individual Catholics to take responsibility before God for their own decisions in life.

Clearly, the Church would prefer and it is ultimately better for individuals if the external and internal fora present a united whole. Those in a second union without having obtained a decree of nullity of the first marriage, for example, may live constantly with some spiritual uncertainty that they may not be at one with God in the new situation.

Hence, the advised solution to these circumstances, if it is possible, is to make use of one of the officially recognised processes, such as a declaration of nullity, so that the second union can be validated. Other solutions that form part of the Church's recommended practice (see for example, Pope John Paul II's Apostolic Exhortation, *Familiaris Consortio*, n.84) are for the couple to recognise the irregularity of their union and to distance themselves from any contradiction with the full practice of their faith. For some couples, this could mean living apart or, if that is not possible, living without that physical relationship that is proper to married couples; the so-called solution of 'living as brother and sister'.

However, for many different reasons, it is not possible for some couples living in an irregular union to use solutions such as living apart, living without that physical relationship proper to marriage, or obtaining a declaration of nullity and having their marriage recognised by the Church. Indeed, many couples in an irregular union do not understand the Church's difficulties with their situation, or perhaps even entered the second marriage not knowing that it was a union that would not be recognised by the Church. Examples of people who might unwittingly find themselves in this position are those who convert to Catholicism whilst in a marriage that the Catholic Church does not recognise, or Catholics who have entered an irregular union at a time of spiritual poverty. However, even those who are spiritually aware might have felt a strong call to enter a new marriage even when, for whatever reason, they have not been able to obtain a formal solution to a previous broken marriage.

The internal forum solution might be of some assistance to those unable to find a solution in the external forum. However, in its strict interpretation, it is not available to everyone in a second union. Nor is it a way to avoid or put aside Church teaching. It is a recognition of the limitations of the various external forum solutions. Since it is a matter of the internal forum, it is first and foremost a matter between God and the couple. The extent of the authority of Church ministers in such matters is limited and is usually restricted to guiding the couple as they attempt to discern the right thing to do. It is the couple, after all, who will have to answer to God for the decisions they made with their lives.

Recourse to an internal forum solution does not mean that an irregular union becomes a marriage recognised by the Church. However, it does effectively amount to a statement that, although the Church cannot give official recognition to the irregular marriage, it is open to the possibility that the parties living in that union are not living a life that is contrary to the gospel.

Hence, an internal forum solution will never include a ceremony of blessing or exchange of consent, or anything that gives the appearance of officially recognising the marriage. Consequently, it is not a perfect solution. It does not resolve the problem of the marriage being irregular but of the inability to receive the sacrament of the Eucharist, which is something that would normally arise from an irregular union.

It is a pastoral solution and it is usually applied only after a period of consultation between the couple and their priest. He will seek to ensure that the couple are properly disposed, that they understand what the solution is and how it will be applied in their particular circumstances and that they have exhausted any possible solutions of the external forum. Without such care being taken, there is a danger that the solution will be seen as dispensing with Christ's teaching that marriage is for life.

The following conditions might be considered necessary for any possible application of the internal forum solution:
- The couple and the priest must be convinced of the invalidity of the first marriage, even though a formal declaration of nullity is not possible, for whatever reason. The minister can rely on the good faith of the couple.
- The parties must be able to receive the sacraments without causing scandal or adverse criticism amongst the faithful.
- The parties must promise to validate the marriage in the event of the death of the former spouse(s).
- The parties must fulfil the responsibilities of Christian marriage in the present union; that is, practice fidelity,

parental responsibility and seek to build an appropriate community of life and love.
- The Catholic party must have continued to practice the Catholic faith as far as possible and, if appropriate, any children of the union should be raised in the Catholic faith.
- The sacraments must be received in a church where the irregularity of the union is unknown, if this is the only way of avoiding scandal.
- The couple must be willing to live without Church approval of their union, even though this does not imply disapproval of their reception of the sacraments.

This is the strict interpretation of the internal forum solution. Clearly it has its limitations. For example, most couples would not be in a position to judge the validity of a marriage, and priests who have not had specialist training are not immune from error when it comes to making such judgements.

It is also difficult to determine when scandal is being given. The danger of scandal arises when a pastoral decision can be misinterpreted as condoning an action that appears contrary to the gospel or Church teaching. However, there can also be a danger that the possibility of scandal is used as an excuse not to apply basic gospel values of love, mercy and forgiveness, when such application might be misunderstood. Such failure can itself be a cause for scandal. The priest can find himself in the position of appearing to condemn a person who has done nothing more than follow his or her conscience, which is one reason that the decision to use an internal forum solution has to be made by the people themselves. There might also be more scandal involved in a couple feeling rejected by their parish community, than there would be in allowing them to receive the sacraments in their own parish. Consequently, those involved in applying the internal forum solution will need to tread warily.

One difficulty in applying the strict conditions for the use of the internal forum solution is that it is not always practicable for these judgements to be made using purely canonical principles. Other more pastoral principles should also be examined, such as the following:
- Were all reasonable steps taken to ensure the success of the first marriage? This is a guide to the respect of the parties for the principles of Christian marriage. It is not an excuse, for example, to refuse the internal forum solution in a case when one of the parties was responsible for the first marriage failing.
- Did and do the parties behave in a responsible, respectful and charitable manner to the former spouse and any children? Is there need for the sacrament of reconciliation before admission to the Eucharist can occur?
- Are the parties living in good conscience regarding the second union; in other words, do they feel at peace with God in their second union? In some instances, there might be need for counselling and/or spiritual direction to enable a proper discernment of their situation.
- Have the parties shown a desire for commitment by at least entering a state-recognised marriage?
- Are they showing stability in this secular marriage and, but for the irregularity of their union, in all other ways giving good Christian example? In other words, does the marriage show external signs of being God-united; are the parties apparently acting under the prompting of the Holy Spirit; does this union give the appearance of having been blessed by God?

- Is the desire to receive the Eucharist a manifestation of a sincere desire for closer union with God?
- Are they giving good Christian example in their behaviour towards others and/or otherwise manifesting their faith by willingness to be involved in the parish community?

This, however, still leaves a problem. The internal forum solution, in its strict interpretation, is not going to help everyone who is in an irregular union and to whom an external forum solution is not available. The Church cannot have a ready answer for all these people. The assumption is that they are breaking the law of Christ, as well as the sixth commandment, and so cannot be admitted to the sacraments.

St Paul tells us: "...neither death nor life, no angel, no prince, nothing that exists, nothing still to come, not any power, or height or depth, nor any created thing, can ever come between us and the love of God made visible in Jesus Christ" (Romans 8:38-39). If, then, nothing can come between us and the love of God, can it be possible for a Christian to find himself or herself in a state of permanent banishment from the sacraments?

In any situation in which a person enters into a state or way of life that is presented as inconsistent with the commandments of Jesus, some contrition might be considered appropriate and this could include some abstinence from the sacraments for a period of time. This might be deemed useful as part of a process of spiritual preparation leading to an internal forum solution.

By way of comparison, it is worthy of note that canon law envisages the possibility of believers committing offences that are considered so serious that the offender is subject to excommunication, either automatically or after a formal judicial enquiry. Formally declared excommunication is more than a temporary need to seek absolution before receiving the Eucharist after committing a grave sin. A formally excommunicated person is not even allowed public association with the Church until such time as the censure is lifted. However, provided certain conditions are fulfilled, there is no reason why full communion cannot be restored.

The offences that justify formal excommunication are far more serious than those that might arise from an irregular union and great care must be taken that there is no confusion between those who are excommunicated and those who are welcome as part of the Church community but do not receive the Eucharist. Excommunication might be imposed upon those who commit heresy, who knowingly desecrate the Eucharist, or who, for purely selfish motives, freely assist in an abortion (but even then, there are often circumstances that mitigate against the application of formal excommunication). These actions are offences against humanity or can cause grave harm to the faithful. When two people are living in a loving and life-giving relationship, the offence of their union being irregular is hardly comparable, assuming there was no great scandal in their coming together.

From time to time, the Holy See has issued guidance to the bishops of the Catholic Church concerning reception of the Eucharist by those who are divorced and who have remarried without Church approval; in other words, those in irregular unions. Obviously, the norms do not apply to those who are simply separated or divorced, as they are not in an irregular union. The general guideline for those in irregular unions is that reception of the Eucharist is not possible.

This guidance, which applies only to situations in which

the first union was a valid marriage, could give the impression of denying the use of the internal forum solution as an appropriate means of helping some of those who are in an irregular union. Such an interpretation is inappropriate, however, as will be explained.

The guidance is restrictive in that it denies the exercise of the right to the sacraments to certain members of the faithful; a right that is acknowledged in the documents of Vatican II (cf. *Lumen Gentium*, n.37). Canon law lays down a principle to be followed in interpreting laws that restrict the free exercise of rights. They are to be interpreted strictly. The guidance issued by the Holy See is not law as such. Nevertheless, because it restricts the exercise of rights, it too is to be interpreted strictly; that is, it will apply only when all the conditions laid down in the guidance are fulfilled. One of the conditions for exclusion from the Eucharist is that the first marriage was valid.

The guidance is based on the assumption that all marriages are valid, but not all marriages are valid. If such valid marriages are God-made unions then they are permanent, and consequently remarriage is never possible as long as the bond of the first marriage remains. However, the Church has no means of knowing God's uniting work in any particular marriage other than by reference to the informed conscience of the spouses. That a couple exchanged vows in a wedding ceremony does not necessarily mean that God has united them. Consequently, if someone can enter a second union in good conscience, which is a condition for the use of the internal forum solution, that person would be effectively expressing a belief that the first marriage was not a God-made union.

Based on Christ's teaching regarding the permanence of

marriage, the Church would state that couples in irregular unions are, by definition, living in a state and condition of life that is not compatible with the Church as a whole. The Eucharist is the sacrament of the unity of the Church and cannot be separated from the sacrament of union with Christ, who is the Head of the Church. For this reason, reception of the Eucharist is inappropriate for those living in irregular unions. However, use of the internal forum solution by a couple after consultation with their priest amounts to recognition that they may not in fact be living in a state and condition of life that sets them apart from the rest of the Church. In such circumstances, reception of the Eucharist would not always be inappropriate. Ultimate responsibility for the use of this solution lies with the couple themselves, as it will be they who will answer to God for the decisions they made in life.

In all of these matters, the Church is concerned that the faithful should not be led into error and confusion regarding the Church's teaching and the indissolubility of marriage. At the same time, there is recognition by many bishops and priests of the need for and use of the internal forum solution and, more generally, a need to give sound pastoral guidance and bring Christ's peace and reconciliation to those wounded by marriage breakdown. This has led to an urgent need to teach the faithful specifically about marriage and the effects of marriage breakdown, but more generally about basic gospel values of love, mercy and forgiveness, as well as the need to avoid judging others (cf. Matthew 7:1).

The use of the internal forum solution conforms with canon law regarding those who may receive the Eucharist. The law recognises that members of the Church have a right to the sacraments but also refers to some who are forbidden by law to receive the Eucharist. Amongst them are those who 'obstinately persist in a manifest grave sin'. Such restrictive canons always have to be interpreted strictly. A manifest sin is a sin that is publicly known. Obstinate persistence would occur when a person continues with the sin refusing to heed warnings from the appropriate ecclesiastical authorities or Church teaching. The canon can apply only when all those conditions are met. Any doubt should prevent use of the canon. The presence of a grave sin has to be established. It has to be manifest, and there has to be obstinate persistence with it. If there is doubt about the application of any of these, the restriction cannot be assumed to apply. Adherence to the conditions for use of the internal forum solution will always leave doubt that the conditions for the application of this canon have been met. In such circumstances, reception of the Eucharist should not be forbidden.

In 2016, Pope Francis indicated some approval with this approach to those in irregular unions in his Apostolic Exhortation, *Amoris Laetitia*, issued after the two assemblies of the Synod of Bishops in 2014 and 2015. This indication, in a footnote of the document, resulted in some controversy, as it was interpreted by some as indicating that the Holy Father was opening the way to all those in irregular marriages receiving the Eucharist. The situation was greatly clarified in 2017 when the Holy Father officially endorsed by letter a statement by the bishops of the Buenos Aires Pastoral Area that had been issued in September 2016. This Spanish letter is published on the website of the Holy See. Translations can be found elsewhere on the internet.

There are those for whom an internal forum solution is not the answer. Many Catholics freely choose to enter a second marriage when the first one breaks down. For some, it is a moment of crisis of faith. They feel they have to make a choice between their faith and second marriage. For some people, when faith seems to stand in the way of personal happiness, it can be difficult to accept that faith is right. Such situations always require careful discernment and openness to the grace of God over a period of time and it may be considered appropriate to follow the example of Christ before his crucifixion when he prayed to God the Father "let your will be done, not mine" (Luke 22:42).

Those who do choose a second marriage sometimes perceive that choice as also involving a decision to leave the Church. It does not have to be so. Some apply for nullity but, in spite of this, for one reason or another, a decree of nullity is not granted. Others simply do not try, feeling that they do not need the approval of the Church to take such a step. If they are living in this second union in good conscience, does the Church have the right to suggest that they are living in a state of sin? Surely, in an individual case, that is a judgement that only God or the individual can make, even if some appropriate pastoral intervention might be necessary if scandal is being given.

The current practice of the Roman Catholic Church is for those who are in irregular unions and who cannot obtain a declaration of nullity to seek advice and guidance from an informed priest who might be able to help them in their quest to resolve any conflict between their faith and their situation in life. Pope Francis has been keen to recognise that discernment in these matters "is dynamic; it must remain ever open to new stages of growth and to new decisions which can enable the ideal to be more fully realized" (*Amoris Laetitia,* n.303). Suffice it to say, there are no easy and quick solutions to these conflicts. Recourse to the words of St. Paul, already quoted in this chapter, might offer some comfort: "Nothing can ever come between us and the love of God" (Romans 8:39).

Glossary of Terms

advocate	one who acts to favour another's cause
auditor	one who hears and records evidence on behalf of the tribunal
bigamous marriage	a marriage entered into while still bound in a legal marriage to another
brief(er) process	a nullity process, introduced by Pope Francis in 2015 that can sometimes be used for manifestly null marriages
canon law	the law of the Church
citation	act of inviting a person to participate in the nullity process
competence	legal capacity of a tribunal to hear a particular nullity application
consent	the act by which a person commits himself or herself to marriage

convalidate	recognise as valid that which was legally presumed invalid
decree of nullity	the formal document declaring that a marriage is null and void
dissolution	the breaking of a bond of marriage
divorce	civil/secular dissolution of a marriage
documentary process	process by which nullity is proved by the presentation of documents
defender of the bond	one who acts to uphold the bond of a valid marriage
external forum	those areas of a person's life that are or can be publicly known; for example, marital status
formal process	full judicial process used to determine if the presented evidence proves that a marriage is null
impotence	the inability to have normal sexual intercourse
instance	a case can be heard in first, second or third instance, depending on whether it is the first, second or third time that judgement is to be pronounced on it
internal forum	matters affecting the conscience and soul and that are not public

invalid	one or more essential legal elements is missing
irregular union	a marriage that the Church does not legally recognise as valid
lawful/legitimate	recognised by the law (whether valid or not)
merely ecclesiastical law	law that is written by the Church for its own purpose and that does not have its foundation in scripture or nature
null	having no effect
officialis (judicial vicar)	the priest appointed by the bishop to run the tribunal in his name
petition	the document requesting an investigation into a marriage
petitioner/applicant	the party to a marriage who requests an investigation to determine if it is invalid
procurator	one who acts on behalf of another
respondent	the (former) spouse of a petitioner
Rota	the ordinary third instance tribunal based in Rome
scandal	that which can cause another to sin (usually the sin of judging another)

sentence	the document that explains the decision of the tribunal
sterility	the inability to conceive children
tribunal	the court established by the bishop to investigate matters of contention
valid	all essential legal elements are in place

Printed in Poland
by Amazon Fulfillment
Poland Sp. z o.o., Wrocław